COUNTDOWN TO CHRISTMAS

COUNTDOWN TO CHRISTMAS

Charlotte Argyle and Taffy Davidson

GIBBS·SMITH
P
PUBLISHER

Salt Lake City

To our husbands and families,
whose love and inspiration brought
this concept to life.

Special thanks to friends and family
who shared their ideas for activities with us, and to
Dallas for his help late at night.

99 98 97 96   6 5 4 3 2 1

This is a Peregrine Smith Book, published by
Gibbs Smith, Publisher
P.O. Box 667
Layton, Utah 84041

Design by Scott Van Kampen
Pattern illustrations by Sharri Cook
Printed and bound in Korea

Library of Congress Cataloging-in-Publication Data
Argyle, Charlotte, 1952-
Countdown to Christmas / Charlotte Argyle and Taffy Davidson.
p.   cm.
ISBN 0-87905-760-2
1. Christmas cookery. 2. Christmas decorations. 3. Christmas stories
I. Davidson, Taffy, 1950- . II. Title.
TX739.2.C45A74 1996
641.5'68—dc20   96-17745
CIP

CONTENTS

THE ADVENT

Counting down the days before Christmas can be fun and educational! In European countries, it is traditional to count the four weeks prior to Christmas. This tradition is referred to as the advent, or the coming of Christ, and starts by counting the fourth Sunday before Christmas.

Another popular way of counting the days before Christmas has been expressed by many Americans in sharing the twelve days before Christmas with loved ones, friends, or complete strangers. In this tradition, we present you with some fun ideas and activities to use with friends and family for these twelve days. We hope that you share the fun, activities and gifts created from this book with those around you. We also encourage you to share them secretly, and then watch the smiles you give to others!

Included in this book are twelve chapters, each dealing with a symbol of Christmas. The chapters contain stories, games, crafts, and recipes. We suggest you plan ahead and choose those activities you wish to use, purchase the needed items early, and then sit back and have fun with your children as you make lasting memories and traditions.

The recipes, activities, and crafts are designed for families. They take adult supervision, but are fast, easy, and fun. Families with older children, or many children, can complete all the activities in a chapter in one evening. Smaller families, or those with young children, can select those things most appropriate.

We have also included instructions for making a calendar to count down the twelve days before Christmas. This calendar has twelve ornaments to reflect the theme for the day. The calendar can be made ahead, or you may want to make the tree ahead and do the daily ornaments as your activity.

The order of the chapters should be left to your family's needs; i.e., the tree chapter would be a fun way to complete the night's activities the day your tree is decorated. Another idea is to assign family members different projects (food, game, craft, story) for the following evening, so everyone shares in the preparation and becomes excited as they wait to see the next theme unfold. Use your imagination, and bring your own ideas to each subject.

We are excited to share these fun family traditions with your family. We hope you will share these treats and gifts with your friends and neighbors, and use them as a tool to teach your children goodwill and the joy that comes from giving. We know that these activities will make your holidays more traditional and will bring cherished memories to each person for a lifetime.

From our families to yours, best wishes this holiday season! ✳

COUNTDOWN CALENDAR

CALENDAR TREE

   1 yd. each 45"-wide felt, red and green

   1 pkg. mini-rickrack, green

   (1) 36" dowel, painted black

   (2) 3/4" black wooden beads, drilled to fit
     ends of dowel

   24 in. 1/4"-wide ribbon

   10 in. 1/4"-wide Velcro, green or black

   Glue gun or tacky glue

   Cut out tree pattern on green felt and center

on red felt. Glue in place. Use rickrack to make boughs on edges of trees (four layers). Glue in place. At bottom of calendar in center, run a 3-inch vertical line of glue. Repeat this between the center line and the outside edges, and again along the outside edge. Turn up bottom of calendar 3 inches to form 4 pockets to hold ornaments. Fold top of calendar around dowel and glue. Put beads on dowel and glue in place. Tie ribbon on each end between beads and calendar edge. Tie 3 inches from center of ribbon to form loop to hang calendar with. Glue 1/2-inch pieces of Velcro onto tree where you want ornaments to hang. Be sure to put one on top of the tree for a star. Apply other side of the Velcro to ornaments.

TREE ORNAMENTS

WREATH

   Felt, lime-green

   Embroidery floss, red

   Embroidery needle

   6 in. of 1/4"-wide lace, white

   Stuffing, polyester fill

   Glue gun or tacky glue

   Trace pattern onto felt, and cut out 2 wreaths. On front of wreath, embroider French-knot clusters of holly berries (4 or 5 sets of 3 berries) with red floss. Glue lace around edge of wreath on back of front. Put stuffing in place and glue back of wreath to back of wreath front. Glue Velcro piece from calendar project to back of wreath to hang.

CANDLE

Felt—white, yellow, lime-green
Embroidery floss, red
Embroidery needle
Stuffing, polyester fill
Glue gun or tacky glue

Trace pattern onto felt, and cut out 1 yellow flame, 2 white candles, 2 lime bases. On front of lime base, embroider French-knot clusters of holly berries (3 or 4 sets of 3 berries) with red floss. Glue base of candlestick onto back of this piece, and do the same for the back of this ornament. Glue yellow flame at base onto back of front candlestick. Put stuffing in place on candlestick and lime base, and glue together. Glue Velcro piece from calendar project to back of candlestick to hang.

SNOWMAN

Felt—white, black, green
Embroidery floss—black, orange
Mini-rickrack
Stuffing, polyester fill
Glue gun or tacky glue

Trace pattern onto felt, and cut 2 black hats, 2 white bodies, and 1 green scarf. On front of white snowman, embroider French-knot eyes (black), buttons (black, if desired), and nose (orange). Embroider a satin-stitch smiling mouth with black floss. Glue rickrack onto green felt scarf to decorate, then glue in place on front of snowman. Slip black hat over head and glue in place. Glue front and back together. Glue Velcro piece from calendar project to back of head of snowman to hang.

GIFT

Felt, white
Mini-rickrack, black
(1) 1/8" or 1/4" cowbell
Stuffing, polyester fill
Glue gun or tacky glue

Trace pattern onto felt, and cut 2 white packages. On front of package, glue rickrack, crossing in middle to wrap. Tie a small bow, attaching cowbell to middle, and glue in middle of package where rickrack meets. Put stuffing in place and glue front and back together. Glue Velcro piece from calendar project to back of package to hang.

BELL

Felt, your choice of color
Mini-rickrack, 1/4"-wide lace,
    pearl beads, or ribbon
Stuffing, polyester fill
Glue gun or tacky glue

Trace pattern onto felt, and cut out 2 bells.

On front of bell, glue lace, pearl beads, rickrack, or ribbon to decorate. Cut 1/2 inch of rickrack and glue on back of top front bell to make small loop. Put stuffing in place, then glue front and back together. Glue Velcro piece from calendar project to back of bell to hang.

TREE

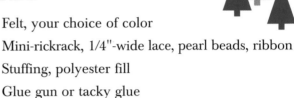

Felt, your choice of color
Mini-rickrack, 1/4"-wide lace, pearl beads, ribbon
Stuffing, polyester fill
Glue gun or tacky glue

Trace pattern onto felt, and cut out 2 ornaments. On front of ornament, glue lace, pearl beads, rickrack, or ribbon to decorate. Cut 1/2 inch of rickrack and glue to the back of top front of ornament, making a small loop. Put stuffing in place, then glue front and back together. Glue Velcro piece from calendar project to back of ornament to hang.

CANDY CANE

Felt, white
Mini-rickrack, red
Stuffing, polyester fill
Glue gun or tacky glue

Trace pattern onto felt, and cut out 2 candy canes. On front of candy cane, glue small stripes of rickrack to give the ornament a candy-cane effect. Put stuffing in place and glue front and back together. Glue Velcro piece from calendar project to back of candy cane to hang.

SANTA CLAUS

Felt—red, white, black, flesh, green
Embroidery floss—black, pink
Embroidery needle
Stuffing, polyester fill
Glue gun or tacky glue

Trace pattern onto felt, and cut out 2 red bodies, 1 pair black boots, 2 green mittens, 1 flesh-colored face, and 1 white beard/hair. Glue flesh face onto back of white beard/hair. Embroider French-knot eyes (black) and nose (pink) onto flesh face. Glue face/beard in center of front of Santa, leaving enough red felt on top to make a hat. Cut small white ball out of felt and glue in place at top of head. Glue top of boots onto bottom of back of Santa front. Glue mittens in place on sides of back of Santa front. Put stuffing in place and glue front and back together. Glue

Velcro piece from calendar project to back of Santa to hang.

YULE LOG

Felt—brown, tan, yellow
Felt scraps, red or orange
Stuffing, polyester fill
Glue gun or tacky glue

Trace pattern onto felt, and cut out 1 tan circle, 2 yellow flames, and 2 brown logs. Glue tan circle onto end of front log. Glue orange or red scraps for sparks in flame on front of log. Glue flame at base onto back of front top of log. Do the same for the back. Put stuffing in place and glue front and back together. Glue Velcro piece from calendar project in center of log to hang.

ANGEL

Felt—white, tan, pink, brown or yellow, black
Embroidery floss—pink, black
Embroidery needle
Mini-rickrack, 1/4"-wide lace, pearl beads, ribbon
Stuffing, polyester fill
Glue gun or tacky glue

Trace pattern onto felt, and cut out 2 white wings, 2 pink bodies, 1 black book, 1 flesh face, and 1 brown or yellow hair. Glue face on to back of hair. Embroider French-knot eyes (black) and mouth (pink) with floss onto face. Glue onto top of body front. Glue rickrack, pearl beads, lace, or ribbon on front to decorate as desired. Glue wings onto back of front; do the same on the back. Put stuffing in place and glue front and back together. Glue book in place in center of angel so she appears to be holding the book. Glue Velcro piece from calendar project in center of angel to hang.

REINDEER

Felt—brown, tan, red, black
Embroidery floss, black
Embroidery needle
Mini-rickrack, white or green
Stuffing, polyester fill
Glue gun or tacky glue

Trace pattern onto felt, and cut 2 tan bodies, 1 brown antler, 4 scraps of black for hooves, 1 round dot of red for nose, and 1 red for saddle. Embroider French-knot eyes (black) with floss on front face of body. Glue red felt nose (or pom pom) in place for nose. Glue red saddle on back of body front; decorate with rickrack. Glue antler in place on back of front head at base. Glue small scraps of black felt in place for hooves on front feet. Put stuffing in place and glue front and back together. Glue Velcro piece from calendar project in center of reindeer's body to hang.

STAR

Felt, yellow
Stuffing, polyester fill
Glue gun or tacky glue

Trace pattern onto felt, and cut out 2 yellow stars. Put stuffing in place and glue front and back together. Glue Velcro piece from calendar project in center of star to hang.

Enlarge by 2X

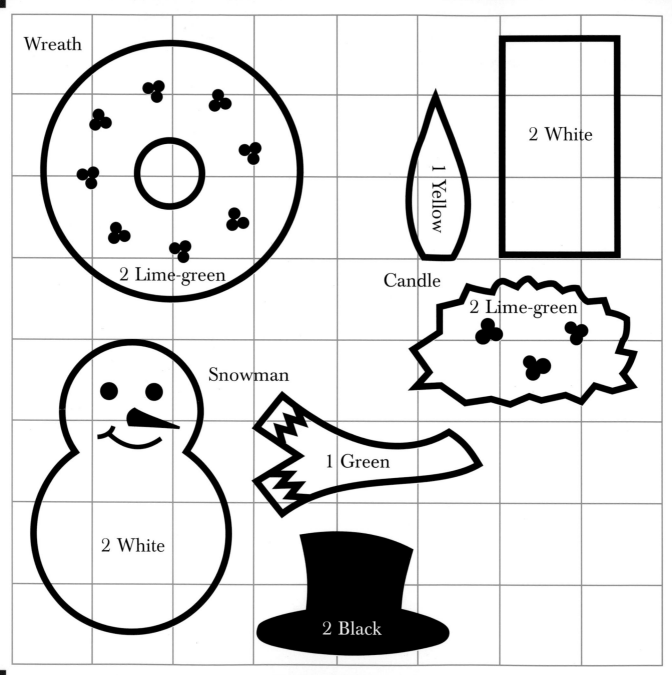

Wreath

2 Lime-green

1 Yellow

2 White

Candle

2 Lime-green

Snowman

1 Green

2 White

2 Black

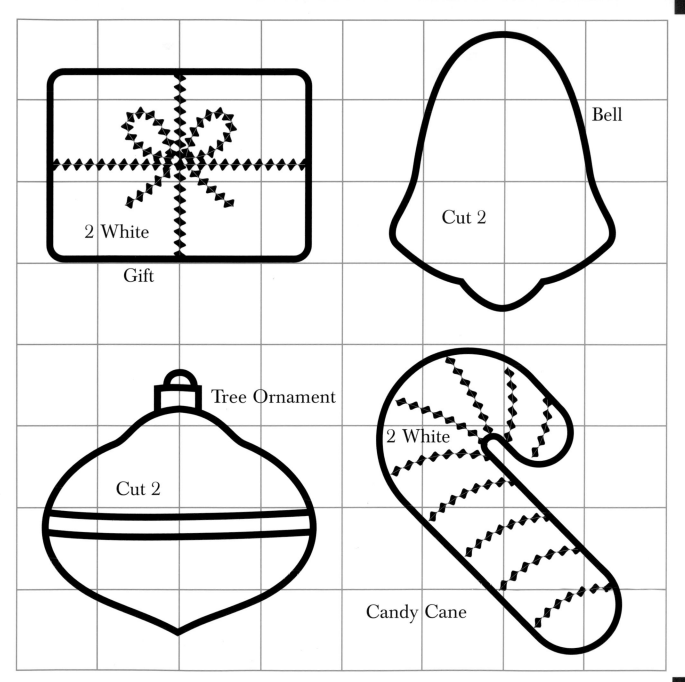

2 White

Gift

Bell

Cut 2

Tree Ornament

2 White

Cut 2

Candy Cane

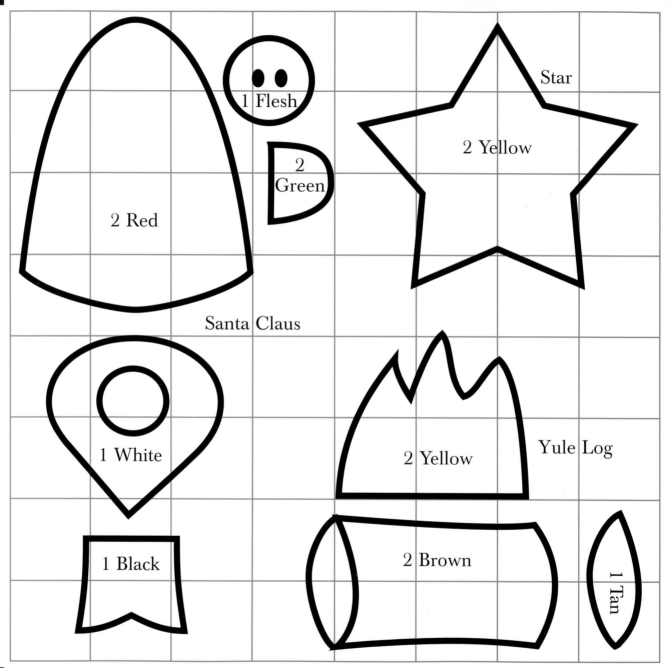

1 Flesh

2 Green

2 Red

Star

2 Yellow

Santa Claus

1 White

2 Yellow

Yule Log

1 Black

2 Brown

1 Tan

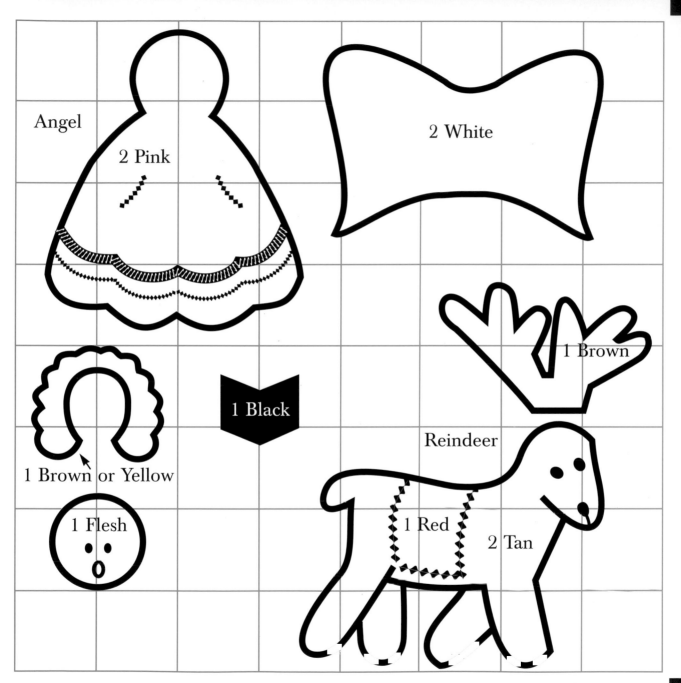

Angel

2 Pink

2 White

1 Brown

1 Black

1 Brown or Yellow

Reindeer

1 Flesh

1 Red

2 Tan

DAY 12 WREATH

A wreath is a symbol of the never-ending nature of love—no end and no beginning. In early times, emperors and rulers wore wreaths of popular green plants around their heads to show they were sustained by the care and love of their people. Christ was made to wear a wreath, or crown, of thorns upon his head when he hung upon the cross. Though forced to wear it out of mockery, the wreath did represent his love for mankind— a love with no end and no beginning, a love for which he willingly gave his life.

CIRCLE OF LOVE

by Charlotte Argyle

Ellen could hear her Mama softly crying. She tried to ignore the sounds by snuggling farther into the soft down quilt, but soon curiosity caused her to creep out of bed and sneak closer to the fireplace to see what her mother was doing. Her mama was sitting in the big rocker Papa had made her back in Kentucky. She was stitching on one of Papa's old shirts, and she would stop often and wipe her eyes on her apron. Ellen silently crept back to bed.

Mama hadn't always been so sad. She remembered how happy Mama was when Papa came home from working hard in the mines, and told her he had finally saved enough money to move the family to Iowa. They would buy a small farm, and with the help of Ellen's two older brothers, they would grow corn and raise cows and make that small farm grow. The family packed, and within two weeks they were on their way to Iowa. The trip had been hard and long, and Papa seemed irritable and not feeling well during most of the journey, but Mama would sing, and make everyone smile. Often she would invent games to play with Ellen to make the time go faster.

Soon they arrived in a small community called Prairieville, and Papa announced they had at last reached their new home. Their farm was about ten miles from town, and had one tree and a small creek running through it. For the first few months, they lived out of their two wagons, but soon Papa and Ellen's brothers, Dallas and Richard, had built a two-room house in the shade of the tree for the family. It wasn't as nice as the house they had rented in Kentucky, but Papa said it was much better because it was their own.

Papa, Dallas, and Richard soon turned their attention towards planting crops so the family would have food for winter and seeds to plant with the following spring. Papa was very ill by then, and he went many times to town to visit the doctor. Soon he spent most of his time in bed, and the doctor came to visit him. Mama said he had gotten very sick from working in the mines. Just before harvest time, Papa died.

Mama no longer sang or played games with Ellen. She was busy helping Dallas and Richard with the harvest. She would help with the milking, and worked day and night doing Papa's jobs and her own. At night she would sit in front of the fire and sew . . . and cry.

The next morning Ellen asked her mother what she was doing with Papa's old shirts. Mama explained that Christmas was coming soon, and since there was very little money, she was remaking the shirts to fit Dallas and Richard.

"Mama, are we going to have a Christmas feast, and tree, and presents, and . . . ?" asked Ellen.

"Now wait just a minute," interrupted Mama. "We don't have the money for all those things now that Papa is gone. We'll have Dallas shoot a goose for dinner, and I'll make a pie, but we won't have the other things." Mama wiped her eyes with her apron.

"What's wrong, Mama?" asked Ellen.

"Oh, I was just remembering the beautiful decorations at the Christmas dance where I met your father," said Mama.

"Oh, do tell me about them!" exclaimed Ellen, but Mama turned and went back to her work.

Outside Ellen could hear Dallas banging on something in the wagon. She climbed up and stuck her head in, but he blocked her way.

"Get lost, or you'll ruin my surprise," cautioned Dallas.

She jumped down, disappointed that Dallas wouldn't let her help him. Richard had a job four days a week in town working for the mill, and he wasn't around for her to bother, so she went back in the house. Mama immediately put her to work kneading the bread dough.

Two days before Christmas, Richard came home from town. Under his arm he was carrying three bundles.

"What are those?" asked Ellen.

"These are presents for my favorite people for Christmas," answered Richard.

"Mama told me we weren't going to have Christmas," said Ellen sadly.

"Nonsense, Christmas comes whether you plan to have it or not," said Richard.

Ellen thought about this, and then realized that was why Dallas wouldn't let her see what he was doing in the wagon. He was making presents. Now she would be the only one without presents for the others. This made her very sad. She thought and thought of things she could buy if she had money, or make if she were older.

Then she had an idea. Bundling up in her warmest clothes, she set out in search of the things she would need to make her special gift for Mama. She was going to make Mama a beautiful wreath, just like the ones they had in past years when Papa was still alive. However, there were no pine trees from which to gather boughs or pine cones. She searched and searched, and then she decided what she would do. She gathered sagebrush, some clean straw from the cows' stall, and some little red berries from the bushes by the stream. Sneaking these into the house, she hid them all under the bed.

That night after Mama finally went to bed, Ellen got up and quietly began working on her wreath. With the help of some yarn from Mama's basket, she soon had made a wreath from the odds and ends she had found. Tomorrow night she would add the finishing touches and make her brothers' presents.

Again, the next evening after everyone was finally asleep, Ellen got up and began working on her presents. She took Mama's scissors and cut squares out of the bottom layer of her petticoat. From these she made handkerchiefs for Dallas and Richard. Using Mama's thread, she finished these off by putting their initials on the corners. Then she took her favorite hair bow, a beautiful gold one that her grandmother had given her, and tied it lovingly around the wreath. Once again she hid these under the bed, and soon she was asleep.

"Wake up, sleepyhead," called Dallas, pulling her out of bed.

"Yeah, it's Christmas morning!" exclaimed Richard.

There in front of the fireplace was a sled Dallas had made for her and a flour box he had made for Mama.

"They're wonderful," said Mama, and Ellen was already sitting on her sled, leaning to the left and then to the right. Richard then handed everyone a package wrapped in brown paper and string. Dallas's contained new work gloves. Mama opened her package and there was a beautiful piece of material.

"There's enough material for new dresses for both you and Ellen," explained Richard. Ellen's small package contained bright-colored candies, which she shared with everyone. Mama then went over to her chest, opened it, and took out the shirts she had remade for Dallas and Richard. Then she handed Ellen a beautiful rag doll, also made from one of Papa's shirts. Her eyes were made from buttons, and her hair from strips of one sleeve. It was the most beautiful doll Ellen had ever seen.

"I told you Christmas would find us," said Richard.

Ellen then jumped up and got her presents from under the bed. Dallas and Richard ooohed and aaahed over their new handkerchiefs, and Mama suspiciously looked over at Ellen's slip hanging on the bedpost. Then Ellen handed her mother the wreath.

"It's a wreath, Mama. It's not as pretty as the pine one in Kentucky, but I was hoping it would make you remember that Christmas dance, and that it would make you happy," said Ellen. Mama took the wreath and began to cry. "Oh no!" thought Ellen. "She doesn't like it, and I've made her sad again."

Then Mama grabbed Ellen and hugged her. "It's the most beautiful wreath I have ever seen," said Mama. She then asked them all to make a circle and hold each other's hands, and she began singing "Silent Night." They all joined in, and they all smiled happily to be hearing Mama singing again. Then looking at her children, Mama said, "You know, this wreath is like our family—a circle of love—with no beginning or ending." ❄

RECIPE
POPCORN WREATH

> 1 pkg. lime gelatin
> 1 C. sugar
> 1 C. white syrup
> 12 red gummy candies (Jujubes, Swedish berries, or gumdrops)
> Popped popcorn (6 or 7 quarts)

Combine gelatin, sugar, and syrup in a saucepan; stir over low heat until all is dissolved. Bring mixture to a boil, and boil one minute. Pour over popcorn and mix together with a spoon. Put into greased round gelatin mold or bundt pan to shape as a wreath. When cool, invert on plate and add candies in clusters for holly berries. For gift giving, add a bright, cheery ribbon.

CRAFT
JEWELED WREATH CARD

> 1/4"-wide ribbon, 7" long
> (1) 7"-by-10" piece of poster board or plain cards
> Carbon paper
> Tacky glue or glue gun
> Green marker

(16) 8-by-12mm emerald acrylic rectangular jewels

(4) 34ss crystal acrylic round jewels

(16) 13-by-9mm red acrylic teardrop jewels

Glue ribbon on one edge of poster board. Fold to make card, leaving bottom of card slightly larger so ribbon shows as edging. Photocopy pattern from book. You may wish to enlarge. Place carbon paper under pattern and on front of card.

Trace pattern with a pen. Remove carbon paper and pattern. Glue back of jewels and place foil-side down according to the shape outline and color code. Repeat until all outlines are covered. Draw in the leaves with green marker. Add your own greeting.

GAME/ACTIVITY
WREATH CHRISTMAS STORY

Players form a circle facing each other. Each player selects a Christmas word such as wreath, reindeer, Christmas tree, etc. Choose someone to be "it"; have him/her stand in the center of the circle and tell a Christmas story. If he/she mentions the word that any player has selected, that player must turn around. At the mention of "Santa," everyone must turn around. The person who is "it" tries to tag another player before he can turn around. If he is successful, the person tagged goes to the middle and continues the story or begins a new one.

DAY CANDLE

Candles were used by ancient Hebrews in celebrating Hanukkah. Ancient Romans used candles in celebrating Saturnalia. This tradition became a part of the Christmas celebration. The candle represents a mirror of a person's inner light, or soul. It is also considered a mirror of starlight and so is a natural representation of the Star of Bethlehem. Just as that star brought light, love, and warmth to the world, a candle brings light and warmth to those who gaze upon it and reflect on the celebration of life.

THE CANDLE IN THE FOREST

condensed from a story by Temple Bailey
published by Ronald Publishing, Montreal, 1933

A small girl and her mother were busy cutting vegetables.

"The onions will be silver and the carrots will be gold," said the little girl's mother.

"And the potatoes will be ivory," laughed the little girl.

"But our tears will be pearls," added the mother, cutting the onions. Again they both laughed.

The next-door neighbor came and said, "What are you doing?"

"We are making a beefsteak pie for Christmas dinner," both exclaimed.

"Well, we are having turkey for our dinner," said the neighbor snidely.

"We are going to have a Christmas pie—we have only a pound of steak to give it flavor, but the onions are silver and the carrots are gold," replied the mother.

"That is nonsense," exclaimed the neighbor. "You both sound silly to me."

"It isn't silly," explained the mother. "I am only trying to make our humble dinner something special for my daughter."

"Enough nonsense. I have come for the rent. Have it ready as soon as possible." And with that, she marched out the door, slamming it behind her.

"Mother, why don't we have turkey?" asked the small girl.

"Because we are content," replied the mother.

"What is content?" asked the girl.

"Making the best of what God gives us; and our best for Christmas day, my darling, is beefsteak pie," replied the mother.

"The boy next door says we're poor, Mother."

"We are rich, my darling. We have love and each other," was Mother's reply. As she held her daughter, she knew the little girl would not get the beautiful doll dressed in pink she had longed for. The money she had saved for the doll would have to pay the rent.

After the little girl had gone to bed, the mother went next door to pay the rent. Inside her neighbor's kitchen, preparations were being made for a large Christmas feast, but fighting and arguing were going on between the woman and her daughter-in-law.

The neighbor boy came to the door and asked, "Are you the mother of the small girl next door?"

"Yes."

"Are you going to have a tree?" he asked.

"Yes."

"Do you want to see mine?"

"That would be wonderful," she replied. He led her to a great room, where a beautiful tree touched the ceiling; and under the tree were toys, candies, and a beautiful doll dressed in pink.

"Will you come see our tree tomorrow morning early?" asked the mother.

"I would like that!" exclaimed the boy. As she left the neighbor's home, she saw the daughter-in-law leaving with her husband and children, suitcases in hand.

That evening, after the little girl's father came home, the mother and father sat up very late, making candy, cracking nuts, and forming balls of popcorn. They cut out funny little fairies from tinfoil. As the mother put all of these into a basket with a red candle, she reflected on the events of the evening and realized she was very rich in the love of her family.

"We will have to get up very early in the morning, and you will have to go ahead and light the candle," the mother instructed the father.

The next morning, the neighbor boy was there before the sun was up. He was invited into the house where a small table was set for four.

"We must eat something before we go out," said the father. At that moment, the small girl came downstairs, eyes aglow with excitement.

"We must eat before we go out," said father again.

"Where are we going?" asked the little girl.

"To find Christmas," was her father's reply.

The boy had a lovely feeling—warm and comfortable—not like what he felt at his home.

After a meal of sweet bread and spicy apples, they went out the door into the woods back of the house. The little girl's father took out a flute and began playing lovely tunes as the little girl and her mother sang. Soon the boy joined in. Suddenly, they came to a clearing, and a hush fell over the woods. There, atop a small living tree, stood a red candle, whose light showed snowy balls and silver fairies.

"It's our tree, my darling," said the mother.

Suddenly, the little boy felt as if his heart would burst. He wanted someone to speak to him this way. He reached out and touched the mother's hand. She looked down at him and drew him close. He again felt warmed and comforted.

At home the boy realized the pink doll had been left under the tree and asked his mother if he could have it. "What does a boy want with a doll?" she asked.

"I'd like to give it to the girl next door. They gave me a Christmas present."

"What did they give you?" When the boy did not answer, the mother said, "Oh, do as you wish."

He wrapped the doll in paper and headed straight to the little house. When the door was opened, he saw the family sitting down to a beefsteak pie for dinner. He went to the little girl and said, "I have brought you a present."

She opened the wrapping and found the beautiful doll. "Is it really my doll?"

The boy answered happily, "Yes."

The mother bent over and kissed the boy. He lifted his face to hers and said, "May I come sometimes and be your boy?"

And she said, "Yes."

The mother watched the boy leave–the boy who knew so little of loving. And because she knew so much of love, her eyes filled to over-flowing.

"And the potatoes were ivory," she said. "Oh, who would ask for turkey when they can have a pie like this?" ✳

RECIPES
BEEFSTEAK PIE

Serves 4

1 to 2 lbs. stew meat or any other beef,
   cut in 1" pieces

3 potatoes, cut in 1" cubes

3 large carrots, cut in 1" pieces

1 pkg. onion soup mix

1 can mushroom soup

1 C. water

2 cans refrigerator biscuits

Combine all ingredients except biscuits and put in a 9-by-12-inch baking dish. Bake for 2 hours at 325 degrees. Remove from oven, and turn oven to 425 degrees. Place biscuits on top of casserole. Bake 10 to 12 minutes, until biscuits are brown.

SWEET PECAN BREAD

4 cans country-style biscuits

1/2 C. sugar

1/2 C. pecan pieces (optional)

1 tsp. plus 1-1/2 Tbs. cinnamon

1 C. sugar

1 cube margarine

2 Tbs. water

Tear each biscuit into 3 pieces. Mix sugar, pecans, and 1 tsp. cinnamon in plastic bag. Drop biscuit pieces into bag and shake. Drop covered biscuits into greased bundt pan. Combine remaining ingredients in saucepan and bring to a boil; then pour over biscuits. Bake at 350 degrees for 30 minutes. Remove from oven; let cool 5 to 10 minutes, then invert on plate. Makes a wreath. Decorate if desired.

CRAFT
JEWELED CANDLE

1 red candle, 3"-to-5" diameter

24 to 48 pronged jewels or colored tacks of your choice

1 Pine bough, 12" to 14" long

Using a design of your choice, push jewels or tacks into candle. Place candle on pine bough for a festive display.

GAME/ACTIVITY
CHRISTMAS SNOOZE

1 candle, lit (use jeweled candle, if desired)

Paper slips (one marked "elf"), folded and placed in a bowl

Place the lit candle on the floor or center of table. Everyone makes a circle around the candle, gets comfortable, and draws a slip of paper from the bowl. The one who draws the slip marked "elf" becomes "it." All lights are turned off so the only light is the dim flicker of the candle. The elf then slowly and secretly winks at a member of the group. This person then falls asleep. The object of the game is for the other group members to guess who the elf is before everyone has been winked at. Take turns around the circle. However, a wrong guess penalizes the guesser so that he has to skip a turn guessing. The elf continues to wink and put others to sleep until his identity is discovered. Put papers in bowl and repeat game.

DAY 10
SNOWMEN

Snow has always been related to the Christmas season, not only because it snows in North America during December, but because the pure white snow represents the hopes and dreams of this season and paints a beautiful landscape to gladden hearts. Snowmen built by happy youngsters are friendly reminders of our childhood and dreams. A big grin, an old hat, and a few coal buttons are all it takes to make the child in each of us laugh in delight.

ONE MAGICAL CHRISTMAS

by Charlotte Argyle

"Another sunny day," exclaimed Talia in disappointment as she ran to her bedroom window. Talia had moved just this year from Idaho to Santa Dias, a small Northern California community. She liked her new house, her new school, and her new friends, but it was December 12, and she missed the snow. Many of her friends had never even seen snow—it hadn't snowed in Santa Dias for seventeen years! What she wouldn't give to be riding a sleigh, building a snowman, or having a snowball fight with her friends.

She quickly dressed and ran downstairs. It was Saturday, and her friends would be waiting for her at the park. Of course, Mom made her sit down and eat a good breakfast (oatmeal, her least favorite), but soon she was at the park and Hillary and Brandy were there, ready to play.

"Where have you been?" asked Hillary. "We have been waiting forever for you."

"Yes, let's go!" said Brandy with a gleam in her eye. "We are going over to bother that old witch—Miss Gray!"

All three girls took off running towards the west end of town. Miss Gray lived in an old run-down house on the edge of the woods, and everyone knew her house was haunted. Its shutters were hanging off the windows, and the weeds had grown up around the house so that you could hardly see it from the road. Besides, Miss Gray had to be a witch. She was old, lived all alone, and always came out yelling and waving a big broom whenever the children bothered her. No one ever saw her in town—not even to buy groceries; so, she must be brewing up whatever she caught in the woods behind her house when she sneaked out at night.

Finally, the girls were close enough to see Miss Gray's house. She was nowhere in sight, so the girls hid just as close as they dared in the trees to the side of her lane.

"Let's throw rocks at her house, and see if we can get her to come out and cast a spell or something," said Hillary.

"I don't know if that's such a good idea," said Talia, hesitantly.

"Oh, come on—it will be fun!" exclaimed Brandy.

The girls gathered rocks and were soon throwing them at the house. Most of the rocks missed, but a few hit their intended target, bouncing off the floors and walls of the porch. "This is fun," thought Talia as she threw a rock with all her might.

"CRASH!" The window by the door exploded.

"Oh no, now you've done it!" said Hillary, accusingly.

The door flung open and Miss Gray came charging out, waving her broomstick in the air. She looked toward where the girls were hiding and yelled, "That's it! I will get each and every one of you, and you will all get what you deserve!"

The girls screamed and ran from Miss Gray's house. Panting, they reached the park. "We're in big trouble now," said Brandy.

"No, just Talia's in trouble," accused Hillary. "She's the one who broke the window. Let's all hurry home so we don't all get in trouble."

Talia didn't feel very well. What if Miss Gray was a real witch and cast a spell on her? What if Miss Gray was just a lonely old woman with no family to help her fix her window? What if she were poor and didn't have the money for a new window? That night, Talia tossed and turned, worrying about the window. All the next day she watched for signs of an evil spell. Then Talia had an idea. She was much too scared of Miss Gray to tell her she broke the window, and she didn't have the money to buy a new one. But what if she took a present to Miss Gray?

Maybe, just maybe, she would forgive her.

Talia's mom had just made some cookies, so Talia fixed a plate of these and headed for Miss Gray's house. She felt queasy, but she knew she would have to go up on the porch, lay the plate down, knock on the door and run in order to make her plan work. As she approached the top stair to the porch, the wood squeaked. She held very still, but nothing happened. She set down the plate, pounded three times on the door, and ran as fast as she could, hiding again behind the trees.

Miss Gray came out on the porch with her broom in hand, looked around suspiciously, then picked up the cookies and walked back into her house, closing the door behind her.

No smile, nothing. But Talia smiled and sang all the way home.

The next day, Talia decided that the surprise gift had been much more fun than throwing rocks at Miss Gray's house. She decided that she would leave Miss Gray a gift every day remaining until Christmas–twelve days, just like the song. She went to the fruit room, found some apples and oranges and again delivered these to Miss Gray's house in the same fashion.

In the days that followed, Talia made Miss Gray a necklace at school, picked her wildflowers, bought a nice apron, and made a cake all by herself. Every day Miss Gray would come out on the porch with her broom, pick up her present, and leave–never smiling once. It didn't matter; Talia would smile enough for both of them.

It was two days before Christmas would finally be here, and Talia had no gift for Miss Gray. She was out of money and there were no treats for her. Tomorrow night she would take her sweet bread, which was a tradition in Talia's home–but what was she going to do tonight? Then Talia remembered that Smokey, her cat, had kittens that were old enough to leave their mother. She picked out the black kitten–her favorite–and just in case Miss Gray was a witch, a black cat was just the thing. She tied a bow around its neck and headed for Miss Gray's house. Again she crept up to the house, placed the kitten down, knocked on the door, and ran.

Miss Gray came out with her broom, took one look at the kitten, and began yelling. "Well, I never–whoever did this will pay!" She picked up the kitten and stormed back into the house.

"What have I done?" worried Talia all the way home.

Christmas Eve came and Talia took the sweet bread to Miss Gray's house. When Miss Gray came out, she was holding the kitten in her arms–not the broom–and she was smiling! Talia ran home smiling even more than Miss Gray had been. That night, Talia slept soundly.

"Talia! Come quick!" Talia woke instantly to her mother's screams. She hurried down the stairs where she could see the excitement in her family's faces.

"Look!" said her father, opening the front door. Talia could see snow falling as she approached the door. "Look there," said her father, pointing toward the sidewalk. At the bottom of the stairs stood a snowman. He had two coal eyes, a carrot nose and a big smile. On his head was an old felt hat, and in his arms was a big old broom–Miss Gray's big old broom! ❄

DOUGHNUT SNOWMAN

3 powdered-sugar doughnuts
   (1 large, 1 medium, 1 small)
1 powdered-sugar doughnut hole
2 mini and 2 regular chocolate chips
1 Red Hot cinnamon candy
1 Fruit Roll-up
2 small red gumdrops
1 large black gumdrop
2 pretzel sticks
1 Oreo cookie (use only 1/2)

Stack the three doughnuts to form a snowman, large on bottom to small on top. Use doughnut hole for head. Use a sharp-pointed knife to make holes in doughnuts for eyes, mouth, and buttons. Place mini chocolate chips for eyes, regular chips for buttons, and a Red Hot candy for the mouth. Put red gumdrops on ends of pretzels for hands; then stick pretzels into doughnut for arms. Cut a 10-inch strip from the Fruit Roll-up and make 3/4-inch cuts on both ends to form scarf fringe. Top snowman with Oreo cookie half and a black gumdrop for hat.

TORTILLA SNOWFLAKES

(12) 6-inch flour tortillas
Oil for frying
Powdered sugar

Heat tortillas in microwave for 1 minute to soften. Fold each tortilla in half, then in half again (should look like pie wedges). Using scissors, cut designs on folded edges much as you would for a paper snowflake. Unfold. Heat 1/2 inch oil in heavy skillet. Fry one tortilla at a time for 30 seconds on each side, or until light brown. Drain on paper towels and cool. Sprinkle with powdered sugar.

SNOWMAN GIFT BAG

Supplies needed:

Gift bag with handles

1/8 yard white fabric

Scrap fabric for hat

1 small bell

2 small buttons

1 silver or black pipe cleaner

1 square tinfoil

Black paint

Orange paint

Paintbrush or toothpick

12 inches raffia

12 inches ribbon

Hot glue gun

Scissors

Trace snowman onto white fabric. Cut out shape and glue onto paper bag. Trace hat pattern (2) onto scrap fabric, cut out, and stitch right sides together along long edges; turn right side out and press flat. Place stream of glue 1/4 from the edge of hat along bottom and about halfway

up both sides, leaving top of hat to hang free. Glue hat to bag. Glue or stitch bell to point of hat. Glue buttons onto front of snowman. Paint on nose (orange), eyes (black), and a squiggly line (black) for mouth. Glue pipe cleaner and tinfoil in place for a broom. Tie a large ribbon-and-raffia bow and glue at the neck.

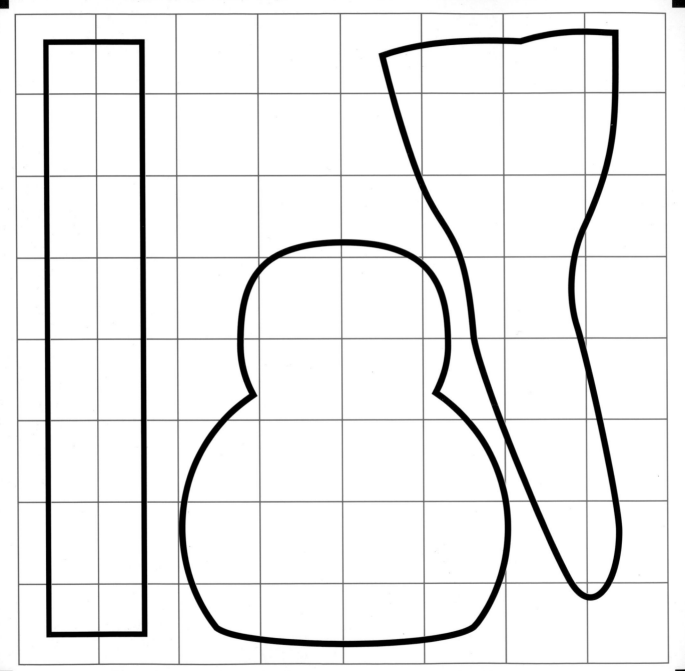

INDOOR SNOWBALLS

40 sheets of newspaper rolled into tight balls
2 baskets (fruit baskets, laundry baskets,
   small garbage cans)
Timer

Be sure to do this where it is roomy and there are no breakables!

Divide into two teams, and divide room into two halves. Each team takes twenty snowballs and one basket. Set each basket equal distances from the dividing line, and place snowballs on the ground to the side of the basket. Set the timer for one minute. Each team begins throwing balls at the other team's basket. When a snowball lands in the basket, it remains there. When it misses, the opposite team may use it to throw at their basket. At the end of one minute, the team with the most balls in the other team's basket wins. Play this several times, and eventually you will have a snowball fight; no one will care about hitting a basket—only each other. ❄

DAY 9
GIFT

Gifts represent our love and feelings toward our fellowmen. They make us feel good when we receive them, but most importantly, they make us feel good when we give them away. Jesus was God's greatest gift to the world. Santa brings gifts to the children of the world. Whether to a next-door-neighbor or a complete stranger, giving a gift is a way of giving a little of yourself. Always remember to tie your gifts with bright-colored ribbon, representing the tying together of hearts in bonds of goodwill.

CHRISTMAS DAY IN THE MORNING

by Pearl S. Buck

Reprinted from *Collier's*, December 23, 1955.
Reprinted by permission of Harold Ober Associates, Inc.

He woke suddenly, and completely. It was four o'clock, the hour at which his father had always called to him to get up and help with the milking. Strange how the habits of his youth clung to him still. Fifty years ago, and his father had been dead for thirty years, and yet he waked at four o'clock in the morning. He had trained himself to turn over and go to sleep, but this morning it was Christmas, he did not try to sleep. Why did he feel so awake tonight? He slipped back in time, as he did so easily nowadays. He was fifteen years old and still at his father's farm. He loved his father. He had not known it until one day a few days before Christmas when he had overheard what his father was saying to his mother.

"Mary, I hate to call Rob in the mornings. He's growing so fast and he needs his sleep. If you could see how he sleeps when I go in to wake him up! I wish I could manage alone." "Well, you can't, Adam." His mother's voice was brisk. "Besides, he isn't a child anymore. It's time he took his turn." "Yes," his father said slowly. "But I sure do hate to wake him."

When he heard these words, something in him woke; his father loved him! He had never thought of it before, taking for granted the tie of their blood. Neither his father nor his mother talked about loving their children—they had no time for such things. There was always so much to do on the farm. Now that he knew his father loved him, there would be no more loitering in the mornings and having to be called again. He got up after that, stumbling blind with sleep, and pulled on his clothes, his eyes tight shut, but he got up.

And then on the night before Christmas, that year when he was fifteen, he lay for a few minutes thinking about the next day. They were poor and most of the excitement was in the turkey they had raised themselves and the mince pies his mother made. His sisters sewed presents and his mother and father always bought something he needed, not only a warm jacket, but maybe something more, such as a book. And he saved and bought them each something, too. He wished, that Christmas he was fifteen, he had a better present for his father. As usual he had gone to the ten-cent store and bought a tie. It had seemed nice enough until he lay thinking the night before Christmas. He looked out of his attic window, the stars were bright.

"Dad," he had once asked when he was a little boy, "What is a stable?" "It's a barn," his father had replied, "like ours." "Then Jesus had been born in a barn, and to a barn the shepherds had come . . ." The thought struck him like a silver dagger. Why should he not give his father a special gift too, out there in the barn? He could get up early, earlier than four, and he could creep into the barn and get all the milking done. He'd do it alone, milk and clean up, and then when his father went to start the milking, he'd see it all done. And he would know who had done it. He laughed to himself as he gazed at the stars. It was what he would do, and he mustn't sleep too sound.

He must have waked twenty times, scratching a match each time to look at his old watch—midnight, and half past one, and then two o'clock. At a quarter to three he got up and put on his clothes. He crept downstairs, careful of the creaky boards, and let himself out. The cows looked at him, sleepy and surprised. It was too early for them too. He had never milked all alone before, but it seemed almost easy. He kept thinking about his father's surprise. His father would come in and get him, saying he would get things started while Rob was getting dressed. He'd go to the barn, open the door, and then he'd go to get the two empty milk cans. But they wouldn't be waiting or empty; they'd be standing in the milk house, filled. He smiled and milked steadily, two strong streams rushing into the pail, frothing and fragrant. The task went more easily than he had ever known it to go before. Milking for once was not a chore. It was something else, a gift to his father, who loved him. He finished, the two milk cans were full, and he covered them and closed them and closed the milk house door carefully.

Back in his room he had only a minute to pull off his clothes in the darkness and jump into bed, for he heard his father up. He put the covers over his head to silence his quick breathing. The door opened.

"Rob!" his father called. "We have to get up, son, even if it is Christmas." "Aw-right," he said sleepily. The door closed and he lay still, laughing to himself. In just a few minutes his father would know. His dancing heart was ready to jump from his body. The minutes were endless—ten, fifteen, he did not know how many—and he heard his father's footsteps again. The door opened and he lay still.

"Rob!"

"Yes, Dad." His father was laughing, a queer, sobbing sort of laugh. "Thought you'd fool me, did you?" His father was standing beside his bed, feeling for him, pulling away the cover. "It's for Christmas, Dad!"

He found his father and clutched him a great hug. He felt his father's arms go around him. It was dark and they could not see each other's faces. "Rob, I thank you. Nobody ever did a nicer thing!"

"Oh, Dad, I want you to know, I do want to be good!" The words broke from him on their own will. He did not know what to say. His heart was bursting with love. He got up and pulled on his clothes again and they went down to the Christmas tree. Oh, what a Christmas, and how his heart had nearly burst again with shyness and pride as his father told his mother and made the three younger children listen how he, Rob, had got up all by himself.

"The best Christmas gift I ever had, and I'll remember it, son, every year on Christmas morning, so long as I live." They had both remembered it, and now that his father was dead, he remembered it alone; that blessed Christmas dawn when, alone with the cows in the barn, he had made his first gift of true love. ❄

RECIPES
CREAM OF MOO SOUP

Makes 3 quarts

(1) 16-oz. can navy beans

6 C. turkey or chicken broth

1 C. onion, chopped

4 garlic cloves, minced

1 tsp. white pepper (optional)

1/2 tsp. crushed red pepper flakes

1/4-to-1/2 tsp. curry powder

1/4 tsp. ground cumin (optional)

2 lbs. turkey or chicken breast, cooked and cubed

1 can white sweet corn

1 C. heavy cream

Green and sweet red peppers, chopped,
   for garnish

Place beans, broth, onion, garlic, and seasonings in a large saucepan. Cover and simmer 15 minutes. Add chicken and corn, simmer 15 minutes more. Just before serving, add cream and heat through. Garnish individual servings with red and green peppers.

OLD-FASHIONED BLACK COWS

Root beer

Milk or half-and-half

Vanilla ice cream

Fill tall glass with 8 ounces root beer. Add 2 ounces milk or half-and-half; stir. Add one scoop of vanilla ice cream.

CRAFT
COW CHRISTMAS CANISTER

This craft takes a few hours to complete, but the result is well worth the time.

1/8 yd. 44"-wide fabric, holiday print

1/2 yd. 44"-wide muslin, white

1/4 yd. 44"-wide fabric, black

1 round oatmeal box

White paper

Tacky glue or hot glue gun

1/8 yd. fusible web

6-strand embroidery floss, dark gray

Embroidery needle

Small paintbrush

Red acrylic paint

Thread, black and white

Polyester stuffing

1 yd. 1/4" ribbon, green

(1) 3/4" cowbell

(1) 1/2" jingle bell

(2) 1/4" black beads

Box: Copy patterns in book. Enlarge if you wish. Cut out material according to directions on patterns. Cut off top of oatmeal box 4-1/2 inches from bottom. Cover box with white paper and cut circle out of white paper for lid. Glue all in place. Cover box with white muslin. Use glue to tack down bottom under box and over top edge. Repeat to cover lid. Cut black spots from pattern, and glue on both sides of box.

Head: Cut out fusible web from patterns for spots on head and pattern for hooves; iron on according to manufacturer's directions for web. Mark head pieces by laying black spots on white face and lightly tracing around them. Mark face on front head piece and mark for

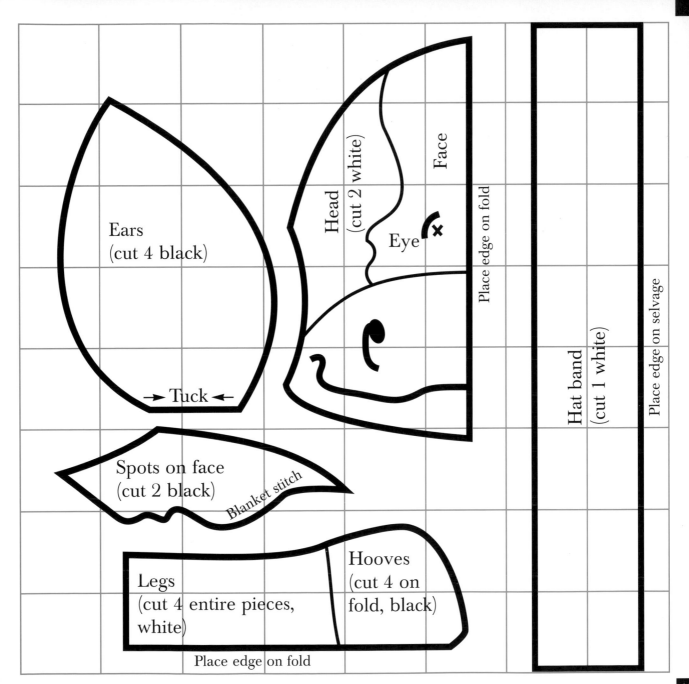

Ears
(cut 4 black)

Head
(cut 2 white)

Face

Eye

Place edge on fold

→ Tuck ←

Spots on face
(cut 2 black)

Blanket stitch

Legs
(cut 4 entire pieces,
white)

Hooves
(cut 4 on
fold, black)

Place edge on fold

Hat band
(cut 1 white)

Place edge on selvage

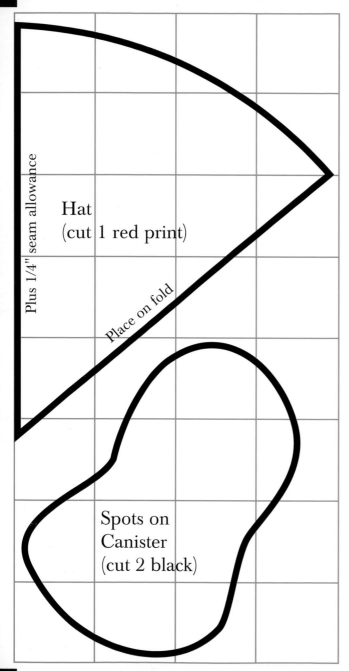

Plus 1/4" seam allowance

Hat
(cut 1 red print)

Place on fold

Spots on
Canister
(cut 2 black)

ears on back head piece. Peel paper backing off spots and hooves, and fuse the spots on the front head piece and hooves to each leg piece as indicated on patterns.

Using three strands of embroidery floss, blanket-stitch across top of each hoof, along curved edge of each spot on face, and across nose. Stem-stitch mouth, eyes, and nostrils. Make a French knot at tops of nostrils, wrapping floss six times around needle.

Color cheeks and chin by dipping paintbrush in red paint and wiping on paper towel until almost dry; then brush lightly on cheeks and chin with a circular motion.

Sew front to back of head with matching thread, right sides together; leave an inch open at top. Stitch ears and legs together in pairs, leaving top edges open. Clip corners on legs, turn right side out, and stuff each lightly. Firmly stuff head and whipstitch opening closed. Stitch beads at markings, going through all thicknesses to back of head and pulling tightly to indent eyes and head. Form a 1/2-inch tuck in the ear openings and hand stitch ears to back of head at marked spots.

Use a running stitch to gather top edges of legs; then stitch legs to back of head at an angle just under nostrils. Hand tack cow head on top of lid.

Hat: Sew hatband onto bottom of hat. Fold hat in half, and stitch center back seam of hat and hatband. Turn right side out and fold hatband up. Cut a 26-inch and a 7-inch piece of green ribbon. Tie long ribbon loosely around cow's neck and over legs, adding the cowbell to ribbon when tying bow at center front. Thread short piece of ribbon through top of jingle bell; then tie ribbon in a bow and hand tack onto tip of hat. Loosely stuff hat and tack to cow's head.

GAME/ACTIVITY
SPOTTED COW GAME

Paper slips, numbered
Gag gifts, brightly wrapped

Preparation: Everyone wraps a gift, either a used item or a joke gift. Wrap it cheerfully and creatively, but do not identify yourself as the giver. Place these under the tree or in a central spot. Make a numbered slip of paper for every member of the group, and place the slips in a bowl.

Method of play: Everyone in the group sits in a circle, then draws a numbered slip of paper. The person who draws #1 selects a package and opens it. He then places his number back in the bowl. #2 is next, and he/she can take either 1) a present from the pile and unwrap it, or 2) any previous player's already-opened present. Be sure the numbered slips of paper are placed back in the bowl after each has been used.

Once each member of the group receives a gift, everyone draws another number from the bowl and the above process is repeated, starting with #1. By this time, all gifts are usually opened, and people begin to take the best gifts from each other. Those with the highest numbers get the best gifts.

DAY 8
BELL

Bells for hundreds of years have served many purposes. Bells call people to worship and prayer. They sound warnings and alarms. They beckon ships to safe harbors. They celebrate birth and new life, and they peal in announcement of death. In all these instances, bells serve as a guide. In the spirit of Christmas, let the bells ring out to guide the lost back to Jesus and serve as a reminder of the love he showed the world.

WHY THE CHIMES RANG

Raymond MacDonald Alden

There was once, in a far-away country where few people have ever traveled, a wonderful church. It stood on a high hill in the midst of a great city; and every Sunday, as well as on sacred days like Christmas, thousands of people climbed the hill to its great archways. The building itself had stone columns and dark passages, and a main room so long, one would scarcely see from one end to the other. In the farthest corner was an organ so clear and loud, it could be heard for miles around. Altogether, no such church as this was ever seen before, especially when it was lighted up for some festival and crowded with people. But the strangest thing about the whole building was the wonderful bells.

At one corner of the church was a great gray tower that rose so far into the sky it was only in very fair weather that anyone could see the top. All the people knew that at the top of the tower were the Christmas bells. They had hung there since the church had been built, and had the most beautiful sound in the world. Some thought it was because a great musician had cast them and arranged them; others said it was because of the great height, which reached up where the air was clearest and purest; however that might be, everyone who had ever heard them thought they sounded like angels far up in the sky.

But the fact was that no one had heard them for years and years. They were Christmas chimes, you see, and were not meant to be played by men or on common days. It was the custom on Christmas Eve for all the people to bring to the church their offerings to the Christ child; and when the greatest and best offering was laid on the altar, there used to come pealing through the music of the choir the Christmas chimes far up in the tower. Some said the wind rang them, and others said they were so high the angels set them swinging. But for many years they had never been heard. It was said that people had been growing less careful of their gifts for the Christ child; and that no offering was brought that was great enough to deserve the music of the chimes.

Every Christmas the rich people still crowded the altar, each one trying to give a better gift than the other without giving anything that he wanted for himself, and the church was crowded with those who thought perhaps the wonderful bells might be heard again. But although the service was splendid and the offerings plenty, only the roar of the wind could be heard far up in the stone tower.

Now, a number of miles from the city, in a little country village where only glimpses of the tower could be seen in fair weather, there lived a boy named Pedro and his little brother. They knew very little about the Christmas chimes, but had heard of the Christmas service. Between them they formed a secret plan to go see the beautiful celebration.

"Nobody can guess, Little Brother," Pedro would say, "all the fine things there are to see and hear; and I have even heard it said that the Christ child sometimes comes down to bless the service. What if we could see him?"

The day before Christmas was bitterly cold, with a few lonely snowflakes flying in the air and a hard white crust on the ground. Pedro and Little Brother were able to slip quietly away early in the afternoon, and although walking was hard in the frosty air, before nightfall they had trudged so far, hand in hand, that they saw the lights of the big city just ahead of them. Indeed, they were about to enter one of the great gates leading to the city when they saw a dark shape in the snow near their path and stepped aside to look at it. It was a poor woman who had fallen just outside the city, too sick and tired to even seek shelter. She would soon be so sound asleep in the wintry air that no one would ever be able to awaken her again. All this Pedro saw in a moment, and he knelt down beside her and tried to rouse her.

Turning her face toward him, he rubbed some snow on it, and when he had looked at her silently a moment he stood up again, and said, "It's no use, Little Brother. You will have to go alone."

"Alone?" cried Little Brother, "and you not see the Christmas festival?"

"No," said Pedro, with a bit of a choking sound in his throat. "See this poor woman. Her face looks like the Madonna in the chapel window, and she will freeze to death if nobody cares for her. Everyone has gone to the church now, but when you come back you can bring someone to help her. I will rub her to keep her from freezing, and perhaps get her to eat the bun that is left in my pocket."

"But I can not bear to leave you and go alone," said Little Brother.

"We both need not miss the service," said Pedro, "so you go. You can easily find your way to the church; and you must see everything twice, Little Brother—once for you and once for me. I am sure the Christ child will know how I would love to come with you and worship Him; and oh? if you get a chance, Little Brother, to slip up to the altar without getting in anyone's way, take this little silver piece of mine and lay it down for my offering when no one is looking. Do not forget where you have left me, and forgive me for not going with you."

In this way he hurried Little Brother off to the city, and blinked hard to keep back the tears as he heard the crunching footsteps sounding farther and farther away in the twilight.

The great church was wonderful that night. Everyone said it had never looked so beautiful. When the organ played and the thousands of people sang, the walls shook with sound, and little Pedro, away outside the city wall, felt the earth tremble around him. At the close of the service came a procession with offerings to be laid on the altar. Rich men and great men proudly presented gifts of jewels and gold. Last of all walked the king of the country, hoping with all the rest to win for himself the chime of the Christmas bells. There went a great murmur through the crowd as the king took from his head the royal crown, all set with precious stones, and placed it gleaming on the altar.

"Surely," everyone said, "we shall hear the bells now, for nothing like this has ever happened before!"

But still only the cold wind was heard in the tower, and people shook their heads and said they never really believed the story of the chimes and doubted if they had ever rung at all. The procession was over, and the choir began the closing hymn. Suddenly the organist stopped playing and the old minister held his hand up for silence. As all the people strained to listen, there came softly, distinctly, swinging through the air, the sound of the chimes in the tower. So far away, and yet so clear the music seemed—so much sweeter than any sound they had ever heard before—that the people sat transfixed. Then they all stood up together and stared straight at the altar to see what great gift had awakened the long-silent bells.

But all that the nearest of them saw was the childish figure of Little Brother, who had crept softly down the aisle when no one was looking, and had laid Pedro's little piece of silver on the altar. ❄

RECIPE
DING DONG DELIGHT

4 individual Hostess Ding Dongs

4 scoops vanilla ice cream

Chocolate Marshmallow Sauce
  (may substitute other topping)

2 C. sugar

1 C. boiling water

1/4 C. powdered cocoa

1 tsp. vanilla

1/2 C. miniature marshmallows

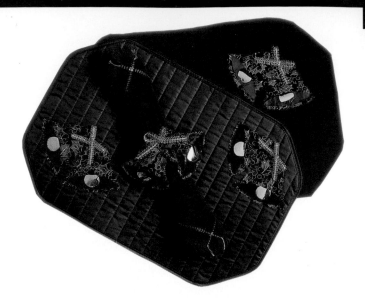

In a saucepan, cook water and sugar to 220 degrees; remove from heat. Stir in cocoa, vanilla, and marshmallows. Cool without stirring until warm to the touch. Beat to thicken.

To serve: put 1 Ding Dong in a dish. Top with a scoop of ice cream and warm sauce.

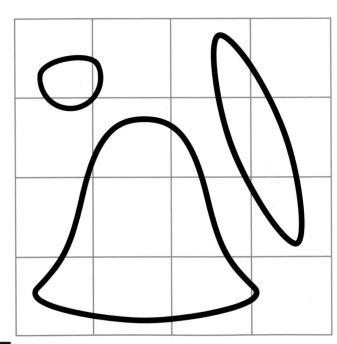

CRAFT
BELL NAPKIN RING
AND PLACE MAT

This plan is for one. Increase yardage for number desired.

1/8 yd. Christmas fabric

Fabric for clapper, solid color

Fabric for inside of bell, solid color

Stuffing, polyester fill

1 yd. 1/4"-wide satin ribbon, your choice of color

1 yd. 1/4"-wide decorative ribbon, gold

1 solid-color place mat

Thread (same color as ribbon)

Pinking shears

Tacky glue or hot glue gun

Sewing needle

Napkin ring: Cut a 4-inch piece of solid ribbon for each ring. Copy pattern and enlarge to desired size. Trace two each of bell pieces on fabric and cut out with pinking shears. Cut out solid clapper and inside of bell from solid fabrics. Glue in place on front of bell fabric. Be sure 1/8 inch of Christmas fabric shows at bottom of clapper. Put small amount of stuffing between two bell pieces and glue edges together. Tie small bows with 1/4-inch ribbon and glue in place at top of each bell. Glue 6 inches of stiff ribbon in middle at back of bell and use to tie around the napkin.

Place mat: Trace bells four times on fabric and cut out with pinking shears. Cut out solid clapper and inside of bell from solid fabrics. Glue in place on front of all four bell cutouts. Be sure 1/8 inch of fabric shows at bottom of each clapper. Overlap second bell on top of first bell. Glue edges of bells down on place mat. Tie small bows with 1/4-inch ribbon and glue in place at top of each bell.

GAME/ACTIVITY
RING-A-LING DING-A-LING

1 bell or bell cluster

Players make a circle, facing each other, standing and holding hands. Select the youngest person to be "it" first. "It" then takes the bell(s) and goes around the outside of the circle, shaking the bell(s) behind each person and saying "**Ring**-a-ling **Ring**-a-ling." He then decides which person should take his place and when he gets to this person, he says, "**Ring**-a-ling **Ding**-a-ling." He then drops the bell(s) behind the selected person and runs around the group. The person he has selected picks up the bell(s) and chases him around the circle. If "it" makes it around the circle to the open space left by the person he selected, then the other person becomes "it" and repeats the game. If "it" gets tagged, he tries again.

DAY 7
TREE

Trees were worshiped in ancient times as the symbol of life. The evergreen, or fir, represents everlasting life and has been called a Christmas tree, meaning "Christ's tree." One night before Christmas, Martin Luther was walking through a forest when he looked up at a stately evergreen sparkling in the light of the moon. He wanted to share this sight with his family, so he chose a smaller tree, took it home, and decorated it with candles and ornaments to enhance its natural beauty and glory.

MY FIRST CHRISTMAS TREE

Hamlin Garland

I will begin by telling you that we never had a Christmas tree in our house when I was a child. But we did celebrate Christmas in those days, always, and I cannot remember a time when we did not hang up our stockings for Santa to fill. As I look back upon those days it seems as if the snows were always deep, the night skies crystal clear, and the stars like frosty sparkles of blue and yellow fire.

We had no chimney in our home, but the stocking-hanging was a ceremony anyway. My parents, especially my mother, were always very merry about it. They always hung their own stockings or permitted us to do it for them—and they always laughed the next morning when they found potatoes or ears of corn in them. I can see now that my mother's laugh had a tear in it, for she loved pretty things and seldom got any during those days.

When I was ten, we moved to Mitchell County, an Iowa prairie land, and there we did well enough that our stockings always held a toy of some sort, and even my mother occasionally received a simple piece of jewelry or a new comb and brush. But a Christmas tree remained the luxury of millionaire city dwellers; indeed, it was not until I was fifteen that I even saw one, and it is about this wondrous event that I write. The land around us was only partly settled at this time, and our district schoolhouse was a bare little box, set bleakly on the prairie. The Burr Oak schoolhouse was not only larger, but it stood beneath great oaks as well. It was our chief social center. There every Sunday morning, a preacher held services, and on Friday nights the young people would meet to debate great questions and read essays. Here it was that I saw my first Christmas tree.

I walked to that Christmas tree across four miles of moonlit snow. Snow? To me it was a floor of diamonds, a magical world, so beautiful that my heart aches still with the wonder of it. Our home at this time was a small frame house on the prairie almost directly west of the Burr Oak grove and, as it was too cold to take the horses out, my brother and I, with our tall boots, our visored caps, and our long woolen mufflers, started on foot defiant of the cold. The snow was deep and we walked in the grooves made by the hooves of horses and the tracks left by the broad runners of the wood sleighs.

Our breaths rose like smoke in the still air, but that did not trouble us in those days, and at last we came in sight of the lights, in sound of the singing and laughter of the feast. It was a poor little building without a tower, and yet it seemed very imposing to me that night as I crossed the threshold and faced the strange people who packed it to the door. I say "strange people" because though I had seen most of them many times, they all seemed like strangers to me that night. I hardly ever came to Sunday school and did not expect a present,

so I just stood against the wall and gazed in awe at the shining pine which stood where the pulpit usually was. I felt awkward and out of place, and even more so when a boy made fun of the way my hair stuck out in every direction. He accused me of having forgotten to comb it! This was not true, but the cap I wore always matted my hair down, and when I lifted it off, my hair always got messed up. It wasn't my fault, but I felt self-conscious and ashamed all the same.

I don't think the tree had many candles, and I don't remember if it glittered with golden apples. But it was loaded with presents, and the girls coming and going wearing bright dresses made me forget my own discomfort. I think I must have stood there for two hours watching every motion as others prepared the way for the great event—the coming of Santa Claus himself.

A furious jingling of bells, a loud voice outside, the lifting of a window, and the dear old Saint appeared clothed in a red robe, a belt of sleigh bells, and a long white beard. The children cried, "Oh!" The girls shrieked with excitement, and the boys laughed and clapped their hands. Then Santa made a little speech about being glad to see us all, but as he had many other places to visit, and as there were a great many gifts to distribute, he guessed he would have to ask some of the many pretty girls to help. They came up blushing and the distribution of presents began. I think now that the fruit upon the tree was mostly bags of popcorn and candy, but as my brother and I stood there that night and saw everybody, even the rudest boy, getting something, we felt sad. We forgot that we had come from a long way off— we only knew we were being left out.

But suddenly, in the middle of our depression, my brother's name was called out, and a lovely girl with a gentle smile handed him a bag of popcorn. My heart glowed with gratitude. Somebody had thought of him; and when she came to me, saying sweetly, "Here's something for you," I could not find the words to thank her. This happened nearly forty years ago, but her smile, her outstretched hand, her sympathetic eyes are clearly before me as I write. She was sorry for the boys who stood so silently against the wall, and her sympathy made the little box of candy a treasure to me.

At last I took my final glimpse of that beautiful tree, and to this day I remember the walk home. My brother and I traveled in wordless companionship. The moon was sinking toward the west, and the snow crust gleamed like a million fairy lamps. The watchdogs barked from lonely farmhouses, and the wolves answered from the ridges. Now and then sleighs passed by with lovers sitting two and two, and the bells on their horses had the remote music of romance to us whose boots drummed like clogs of wood upon the icy roads. Our house was dark as we approached and entered it, but how deliciously warm it seemed after the sharp, cold wind! I admit we headed straight for the cupboard for a piece of mincemeat pie and a glass of milk!

As I write this, there stands in my library a thick-branched fir tree covered with gold and purple apples, together with crystal ice points, green and red and yellow candles, clusters of gilded grapes, wreaths of metallic frosts and glittering angels; but I doubt that my children will ever know the deep pleasure which came to my brother and me in those Christmas days when an orange was not a fruit but a rare treasure from a warm, faraway land.

That was all we had—few possessions and a deep appreciation. And the lesson of it all is, if we are looking for a lesson, that it is better to give to those in need than to those with much who simply expect to get something as a matter of course. ❋

RECIPE
STANDING CHRISTMAS TREE COOKIES

1-1/2 C. softened margarine

1 C. sugar

1 egg

2 tsp. vanilla

Green food coloring

4-1/2 C. flour

1/2 tsp. salt

1 tsp. cinnamon

1/4 tsp. ginger

1 container white icing

Mix margarine and sugar, beating at high speed until fluffy. Add egg, vanilla, and a few drops of green food coloring. At low speed, beat in flour, salt, cinnamon, and ginger—half at a time. Chill until firm enough to roll out. Take quarter of dough and roll out to 1/8 inch thick. Using a 3- to 5-inch tree-shaped cookie cutter, cut out cookie shapes, cutting off trunks. Cut one-half of trees in half lengthwise. Bake at 375 degrees for 7 to 10 minutes; let cool. Decorate with icing and candy toppings if desired. Spread thick frosting on edge of each tree half. Press one tree half onto center of

each side of each whole tree, so that tree will stand on its own. Let stand to dry completely.

CRAFT
PINE-CONE FIRE STARTERS

2 boxes paraffin wax

Electric frying pan or double boiler

1 to 4 crayons, green or red, for color

3 drops pine-scented oil (if desired)

Muffin tin

5"-long wicks (string dipped in paraffin)

Tongs

Pine cones (approximately 2-1/2" to 3" in diameter)

Decorative basket

Creative Twist Ribbon (twisted crepe)

Melt paraffin in electric frying pan or double boiler. CAUTION: Do not use paraffin around an open flame or over an electric burner. Add 1 to 4 crayons for color (1 for light color, up to 4 for darker) and scented oil. Grease muffin tin, and fill each cup half full of melted paraffin wax. Place a wick in cup, leaving half of wick hanging over top edge. Using tongs, dip pine cones in wax to cover, then set upright in muffin tins. Allow paraffin to harden. Decorate basket as desired, adding large bow. Fill with fire starters. For gift giving, give these instructions: *Place a few fire starters under logs and light wicks.*

GAME/ACTIVITY
HOT CHESTNUTS

Chestnuts (or substitute another
        nut or object)
Christmas music

Everyone sits in a circle facing each other. The object of the game is to begin the music and pass the "hot" chestnut around the circle. One person controls the music and, keeping his/her back to the circle, stops the music randomly. The person caught with the hot chestnut when the music stops must move out of the circle. The last person left in the circle is the winner.

DAY 6
CANDY CANE

The tastes of Christmas are part of all our memories, and one of the favorite of these is candy canes. Not only are they flavorful but, as decorations on trees, they bring color and reflect light.

The candy cane is shaped like the crooked staff used by the shepherds of old to bring their lambs safely home. This same staff was carried by shepherds who visited baby Jesus. At this special time of year, we hold onto the staff, bringing us closer to the safety and shelter of the manger.

THE SWEET GIFT OF CHRISTMAS

by Charlotte Argyle

Michael lay on the soft grass, gazing dreamily at the fluffy clouds and trying to make lambs out of their various shapes. Someday he was going to own his own flock, and he was going to have as many sheep as there were clouds in the sky, but for now he had to be satisfied being a shepherd and learning the care and keeping of those sheep and lambs assigned to him. Slowly he drifted off to sleep, smiling contentedly to himself.

"Bleat! Bleat!" Michael's sleep was abruptly ended by a loud, sorrowful cry from one of his sheep. Regaining his senses, he looked around, quickly taking a head count of his flock. All sheep were accounted for, but one old ewe was bleating loudly. As he approached the ewe, he realized her problem—her two-week-old lamb was missing from her side. Once again he went through the flock, trying to find the missing lamb, but to no avail.

Grabbing his staff, he walked the short dis-tance to the ridge where the sheep had been grazing earlier that morning. As he approached the edge of the ridge, he could hear a small bleat coming from below. He looked over the edge, and there on a small shelf of rock about four feet below him was the small lamb. She appeared to be alright, but she was shaking with fear.

Michael looked for a way down so that he could reach the lamb, but there was none. So, holding his staff tightly, he leaned over the ledge as far as he could, and gently wrapped the crook of his staff under the lamb's small stomach, right behind the lamb's front legs. Slowly he raised the staff, holding his breath and hoping the staff would not break. He had found the stick for his staff when he first became a shepherd two years ago. Many of the other shepherd boys had made fun of his staff, telling him it was too long, too thin, not strong enough, and funny looking because of its large crooked handle. Most of them had straight, strong sticks. Today he was glad his stick had a deep crook. Now he just hoped it would be strong enough to lift the lamb.

Slowly and gently he pulled the staff up. The staff creaked and moaned, but soon he had the small, shaking lamb in his arms. Grasping the staff, he proudly ran back to his flock and set the lamb down by its grateful mother.

Michael rounded up his sheep and headed for the camp. His stomach was growling and he knew it was time for dinner. He couldn't wait to tell his best friend, James, about his exciting day. Soon the camp was in sight, and James came running out to meet him. In no time at all, it was all over camp that Michael had saved a lamb with his odd staff. Many of the shepherds came by and poked fun at Michael and his staff as he sat and ate. He was used to their teasing and ignored them.

After dinner, James pulled out his flute and began playing beautiful tunes as many of the shepherds gathered around. Michael thought James' flute was the best thing in the world. James' mother had given it to him when he left home to become a shepherd. Michael's mother had given him a red sash when he left home, and he wore it around his tunic. She had made it and it was nice, but he would much rather have had a gift like James' flute. Maybe then the other shepherds wouldn't tease him but would listen to him as they did to James.

Suddenly James quit playing his flute in the middle of a tune. One by one the shepherds stood up and pointed toward the skyline. There was a bright light where they pointed, and soon all were staring in awe at a beautiful angel. Soon the angel was surrounded by other angels and they all were singing. Michael and the other shepherds fell on their knees, hiding their faces in fear. The first angel then spoke.

"Fear not, for I bring you good tidings of great joy, for unto you is born this day, in the city of David, a savior, which is Christ the King."

Slowly the angels disappeared, and the shepherds rose from where they had fallen. On the horizon, a large bright star had replaced the angels. In quiet tones the shepherds discussed traveling to Bethlehem with gifts for the new king. In excitement they all rushed around gathering their prize possessions. Some gathered lambs, some treasures of cloth and jewelry.

"What are you going to give the new king?" Michael asked James. "I think I will play him a song on my flute," answered James. "Everyone enjoys my music, and I'll give him the new song I have been working on. What are you going to give him?"

"I will give him my staff," said Michael. "It

has proven itself to be good and strong." James smiled at this, and Michael thought maybe this was not such a good idea if his best friend thought it was a funny gift. He began to worry because he had nothing else to offer the new king.

The shepherds soon were on a hill overlooking the city of Bethlehem. Below them on the outskirts of the city stood a small stable, above which the star glowed brightly. Cautiously, the shepherds approached the stable. There in the warmth of the stable's straw lay a beautiful woman with a small baby in her arms. A man approached the shepherds, introduced himself to them as Joseph, and invited them to come closer and view the new baby. No one had to ask who this child was; everyone present knew this was the Savior of the world who had come to fulfill ancient prophecies.

One by one shepherds and other strangers who had gathered approached the baby, laying gifts beside his manger. James and other musicians played their wonderful songs for the new king. Michael suddenly felt embarrassed by his gift. All the other boys had made fun of his staff, even after he had told them his heroic tale. What could he possibly be thinking? What would a baby or a king, for that matter, want with an old shepherd's staff? In embar-

rassment, he removed his sash from around his waist and began wrapping it around his staff, trying to hide it from everyone's sight. Maybe he should just run away now, but he so wanted to see this baby, with or without a gift.

His time to approach the manger had come. Slowly he walked up to the baby, hiding his cane and sash behind him. What a beautiful baby! This was indeed a king. At that moment, the baby's mother stood up and took a step towards Michael, her hand outstretched. He reluctantly handed her the staff, still wrapped in the red sash.

"It is beautiful!" exclaimed the baby's mother. "My son will use this staff to lead his lambs back to his father in heaven." Michael walked away in stunned silence.

Years passed, and Michael finally owned a large flock of sheep. He found another staff–this time straighter–but he knew it wasn't as strong. He often wondered if the beautiful lady had kept his funny staff that night, or if she was only being nice, throwing it away after he left.

He heard that the new king was passing through the countryside where he lived. It had been almost thirty years since that wonderful night when Michael had visited the stable, so he hurried to the roadside to see the king. As he watched, a large procession of people came walking up the dusty road. He saw they were being led by a handsome young man carrying a staff with a red sash wrapped around its deep crook–the same staff and sash given in love on that night so long ago. ❄

RECIPE
VERY-BERRY CANDY-CANE APPETIZER

   3 C. frozen red berries
     (cranberries, raspberries, or strawberries)
   3/4 C. brown sugar
   1/3 C. water
   1/8 tsp. allspice
   1/8 tsp. cloves
   1/8 tsp. ginger
   1/8 tsp. dry mustard
   (3) 8-oz. pkgs. cream cheese

Mix the berries, sugar, water, and spices in a saucepan. Cook and stir over medium heat for 7 minutes. Drain excess liquid. Cool. Shape cream cheese into a candy cane. Spoon out troughs where you want to add stripes, then fill troughs with berry mixture. Serve with crackers, fruit, bagels, or toast.

CRAFT
CANDY-CANE CANDLEHOLDER

   Hot glue gun
   6 large candy canes
   (1) 10"-to-12" tapered candle
   Miniature ornament
   (1) 12" piece of ribbon
   Small piece of silk holly

Glue 3 candy canes evenly in place around tapered candle, with crooks at the bottom. These become the base of the candleholder. Turn candle upside down and glue 3 candy canes between the others with crooks toward the wick. Thread miniature ornament on ribbon and tie ribbon around candy canes and candle. Be careful not to tie too tight or canes will pop off. Glue holly to candle near ribbon.

GAME/ACTIVITY
CANDY-CANE RELAY

2 candy canes
2 balloons, inflated

Divide into two teams and decide on a common goal line. Each team lines up and begins the race. The object of the game is to balance the balloon on a candy cane and hurry to the goal line and back. If the balloon falls off, it must be replaced on the candy cane before continuing the race.

DAY 5
SANTA CLAUS

Nicholas of Myra and Nicholas of Pinor, known in fourth-century Holland for their good deeds, were combined into one symbol—St. Nicholas, a man who left gifts in wooden shoes for boys and girls. From England came Father Christmas, who was jolly and round and wore tall boots. Germany provided Kris Kringle, who helped the Christ Child bring gifts to deserving people. Today, qualities of all of these figures are combined, bringing the best of each to our Santa Claus—a symbol of unselfish giving.

IS THERE A SANTA CLAUS?

by Francis P. Church

an editorial from the *New York Sun,* September 21, 1897

Dear Editor:

I am eight years old. Some of my little friends say there is no Santa Claus. Papa says, "If you see it in 'The Sun' it's so." Please tell me the truth, is there a Santa Claus?

Virginia O'Hanlon
115 West 95th Street
New York City

Virginia, your little friends are wrong. They have been affected by the skepticism of a skeptical age. They do not believe except they see. They think that nothing can be which is not comprehensible by their little minds. All minds, Virginia, whether they be men's or children's are little. In this great universe of ours man is a mere insect, an ant, in his intellect, as compared with the boundless world about him, as measured by the intelligence capable of grasping the whole of truth and knowledge.

Yes, Virginia, there is a Santa Claus. He exists as certainly as love and generosity and devotion exist, and you know that they abound and give to your life its highest beauty and joy. Alas! How dreary would be the world if there were no Santa Claus! It would be as dreary as if there were no Virginias. There would be no childlike faith, then, no poetry, no romance to make tolerable this existence. We should have no enjoyment, except in sense and sight. The eternal light with which childhood fills the world would be extinguished.

Not believe in Santa Claus! You might as well not believe in fairies. You might get your papa to hire men to watch in all the chimneys on Christmas eve to catch Santa Claus, but even if they did not see Santa Claus coming down, what would that prove? Nobody sees Santa Claus, but that is no sign that there is no Santa Claus. The most real things in the world are those that neither children nor men can see. Did you ever see fairies dancing on the lawn? Of course not, but that's no proof that they are not there. Nobody can conceive or imagine all the wonders there are unseen and unseeable in the world.

You tear apart the baby's rattle and see what makes the noise inside, but there is a veil covering the unseen world which not the strongest men that ever lived, could tear apart. Only faith, fancy, poetry, love, romance, can push aside that curtain and view and picture the supernal beauty and glory beyond. Is it all real? Ah, Virginia, in all this world there is nothing else real and abiding.

No Santa Claus! Thank God he lives, and he lives forever. A thousand years from now, Virginia, nay, ten times ten thousand years from now, he will continue to make glad the heart of childhood. ❄

RECIPE
KRIS KRINGLE KRUNCH

3 C. puffy corn cereal, presweetened

3 C. flake rice cereal, unsweetened

2 C. nuts

2 C. colored miniature marshmallows

1-1/2 lbs. dark or white chocolate

Mix dry ingredients. Melt dark chocolate on low in microwave or over a double boiler. Pour over all and stir. Cool and break into chunks.

CRAFT
SANTA DOOR HANGER

3/4 yd. each of felt–green, red, white

1/4 yd. felt, flesh-colored

8"-by-1" piece of felt, white

Stuffing (batting or your choice)

(2) 12mm eyes

(1) 1/2" pom-pom, black

Stuffing of choice for beard, white

(3) 7' lengths of jute

Cardboard or poster board

(1) 1" jingle bell

(1) 2" jingle bell

1 bow made of Christmas ribbon

Use flesh-colored felt and cut out pattern of face. Cut out 3 "H"s and 3 "O"s on cardboard. Using green felt, cut out 2 "H"s and 1 "O." Using red felt, cut out 1 "H" and 2 "O"s. Make sure that felt "H"s and "O"s are 1/4-inch larger all around the pattern. Fold red felt and cut out

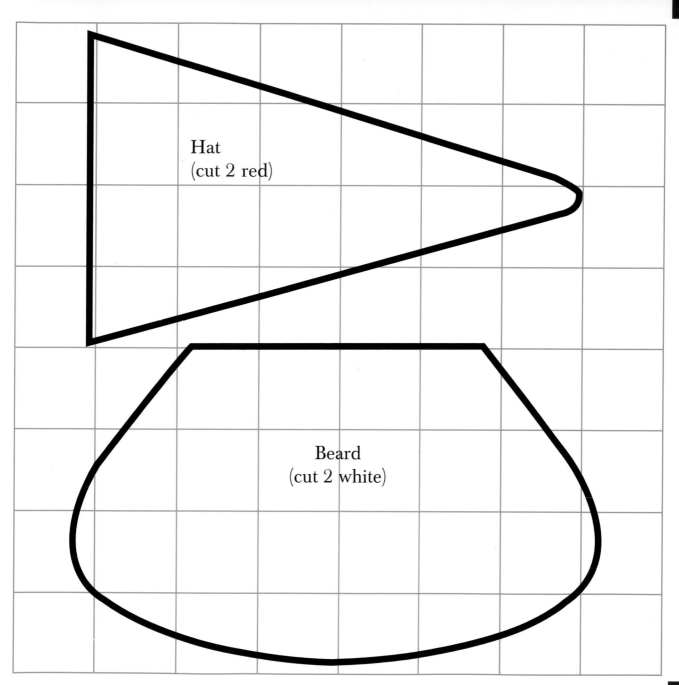

Hat
(cut 2 red)

Beard
(cut 2 white)

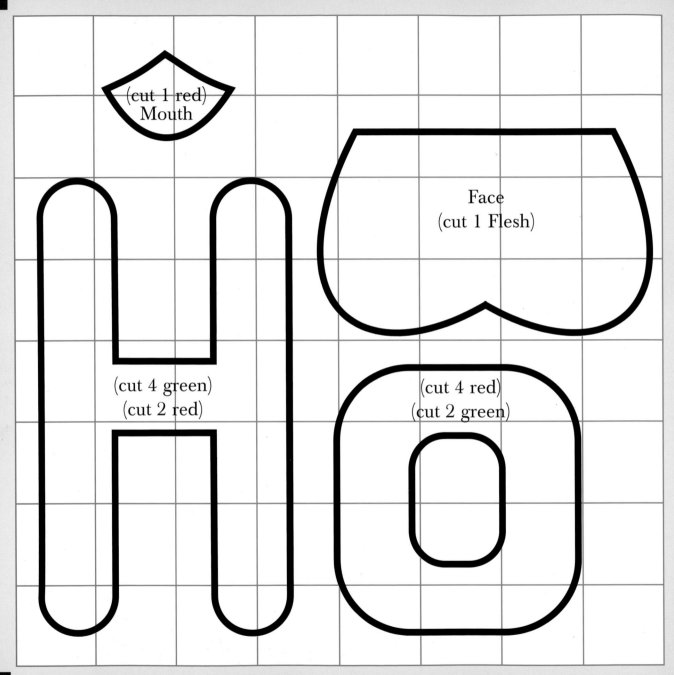

(cut 1 red)
Mouth

Face
(cut 1 Flesh)

(cut 4 green)
(cut 2 red)

(cut 4 red)
(cut 2 green)

hat and mouth patterns. Glue "H"s and "O"s onto cardboard, alternating colors. Then glue "O"s onto front side of "H."

Cut out beard. Stuff cheeks of face and glue onto beard, matching straight line. Then glue mouth, eyes, nose, and stuffing on beard and face as mustache. Glue completed front face and beard onto white back, stuff as desired. Glue hat on head and bell on top of hat. Cut out strip of white felt to decorate hat.

Braid three strands of jute together. Leave loop at top for hanging and four inches at bottom. Fray at bottom. Attach large bell near bottom.

Hot glue pieces to jute: head at top, three "Ho"s down braided rope. Glue bow at top near loop for hanging.

GAME/ACTIVITY
HO! HO! HO!

Everyone sits in a circle facing each other. Have one person say "HO!"; the second person says, "HO! HO!"; the third person says, "HO! HO! HO!"; this continues all around the circle. The "HO!"s must be said without laughing. Anyone laughing is out of the game; the last one remaining is the winner.

DAY 4
YULE LOG

The Yule log comes from an old Scottish tradition around the Christmas fire. Care was taken in selecting the best log for this special night, because it symbolized promises for a wonderful, bright future. This log had been growing for hundreds of years, storing up sunshine and energy from the spirits living in the forest. All of these were released when the log was burned in the fire, brightening the homes and lives of those who were present.

SPIRITS OF THE YULE LOG

by Charlotte Argyle

Fifty years had passed, and still Dacquiri could remember that Christmas as if it were yesterday. She had only been nine at the time, and her brother, Robert, was twelve. They lived in the French countryside on a small farm with their mother and father. Young Dacquiri had always thought of her home as a beautiful, quiet place, but in recent months, that had changed. The Germans and Americans were fighting. Both countries felt that they needed France—more particularly, Paris—in order to win the war. Dacquiri's family did not support either side of the war; all they wanted was for everyone to go away and let them get on with their normal lives. But the war had dragged on, many soldiers on both sides had lost their lives, and the beautiful countryside was slowly being destroyed.

As the fighting grew closer, Father and Robert took turns in the evenings keeping watch over the livestock and the family home. Father was extremely nervous about the fighting and was afraid that his family might be dragged into the middle of the war or their belongings confiscated for the soldiers' needs.

Then, one day, the German soldiers came through and told Dacquiri and her family that they would be arrested if they were found helping the American soldiers. Father reassured them that his family only wanted to be left alone and did not support either side.

A few days before Christmas, Father received word that his mother in Paris was very ill, and he had to make arrangements to see her before she died. He gathered the family and told them of his plans. He was very worried about leaving his family while the fighting was going on so close by, but he had to help his mother. Before he left, he and Robert shot a big goose for Christmas dinner.

In addition, Father brought home a large round log to be burned Christmas Eve. This yule log was so big that it barely fit in the fireplace. Father reassured them that this log would burn all night and give off forest spirits that would protect them from harm while he was away. Of course, he had told them this with a twinkle in his eye, but Dacquiri believed every word of it.

Christmas Eve day arrived, and everything was going well for the small family. Mother and Dacquiri were making preparations for tomorrow's feast; they had made sweet breads and a pot of stew for this evening's supper. Robert had taken care of the chores, cut kindling for the fire, and found enough time to cut down a small Christmas tree for the family.

Evening came, and Robert started the yule log burning. Mother put a pot of stew on the hanger above the fireplace, and then she popped some popcorn to string for the tree. While Mother and Robert worked on the popcorn, Dacquiri made ornaments out of paper and buttons. As the yule log crackled in the fireplace, everyone began to feel the warm spirit of the holiday. Then a knock came at the door.

Mother walked slowly, hesitantly, toward the door. They were expecting no visitors, and they had heard gunfire all day. None of their friends or neighbors would be out on a night like this. She slowly opened the front door. Standing there were two American soldiers. One was wounded and was being held up by the other. The unwounded soldier then spoke to Dacquiri's mother in broken French.

"We are lost, and my friend here is hurt. Can you please help us?" he pleaded.

"No, no . . . please go. We are alone here and can't help you," answered Mother.

"We will go then. We just thought that maybe you would be kind and feed us and let us get warm and rested," said the soldier, turning away with his hurt companion.

Mother then threw the door wide open and reached for the soldier who had spoken to her, exclaiming, "Hurry, Robert, help me get these two in by the fire."

Robert helped the wounded soldier lie down by the fire, and Dacquiri pulled her father's chair closer to the fire for the other soldier. Mother then directed Robert to take the soldiers' guns out to the barn, explaining to them that she would not allow guns in her home.

Mother took some clean cloths and began working on the wounded soldier's shoulder. He had been shot, and the bullet was lodged in his shoulder. She cleaned the wound and bound it, hoping the bleeding would soon stop. Then she fed the soldier some stew broth until he drifted asleep. Dacquiri fixed the other soldier a bowl of stew and broke off some bread for him. Robert nervously paced back and forth, eying the soldiers suspiciously and mumbling under his breath.

"Your fire is beautiful and warm," said the soldier. "It reminds me of my home and my family. And you, little lady, remind me of my girlfriend. You know, she has eyes just the same color of hazel as yours." Dacquiri giggled, and Mother smiled.

"It's our yule log that makes everything so warm," said Dacquiri. "It gives off spirits of animals and fairies from the woods. Father said it will keep us safe from the fighting and from the soldiers." She blushed as she realized what she had just said. The soldier laughed, and then they all laughed together.

"Ssshhh!" quieted Robert, who was peeking out the window by the door. "I see someone coming towards the house." Then there was a knock at the door. Mother motioned for Dacquiri to help her put a blanket over the wounded soldier, and she led the other soldier into the back room. Adjusting her apron, Mother slowly opened the front door. There on the porch stood a tall, young German soldier.

"What can I help you with?" asked Mother. The soldier shook his head. "Do you speak French?" Again the soldier shook his head. Mother motioned for Robert to come to the door, and Robert asked him in his best German what he wanted. The soldier then said something to Robert, and he turned and said, "Mother, he says he is lost and cold and needs our help."

Mother stood there for a moment gazing at the fire, looking for its magical answer to this problem. Then she said to Robert, "Explain to him that he can come in and eat and get warm, but he must accept our other guests. Also explain to him that you must have his gun to put in the barn." Robert conveyed this message as best he could to the German soldier. After a moment's silence, the soldier handed Robert his gun. Mother stepped aside and let the soldier in. She had him sit in her chair close by the fire.

Dacquiri brought the American soldier back into the room. Immediately the German soldier stood up and acted as if he were going to strike the American. Mother stood between them. She explained in French to the

American soldier while Robert explained in German to the other soldier that they were both guests in her home, it was Christmas Eve, and she had taken them in to feed them, warm them, and help heal them. She did not care about the battle; there would be plenty of time for that another day, somewhere else. Both soldiers sat down, each watching the other. Dacquiri ladled stew and broke bread for the new soldier. He was obviously starving, and soon she was fixing him another bowl.

Mother again went to work on the wounded soldier. The German soldier came over to her side, took out a small medical bag from his pack, and began helping her. Mother smiled at him and said, "Danka."

Later that evening, the soldiers spoke of their homes, girlfriends, and families. Mother and Robert interpreted for all to understand. Dacquiri was asked by the American soldier to repeat her story of the yule log to the German soldier. They laughed together, and both soldiers made wishes to the family of peace and love.

Dawn soon broke the night skies, and Mother fixed each soldier a bag with bread and meat in it. The wounded soldier was now able to get up and move around, and the bleeding had completely stopped, thanks to the German soldier's help. The Americans shared the whereabouts of the German line with their new friend so that he could return there safely. Each soldier shook hands with Robert, kissed Dacquiri on the cheek, and hugged Mother, thanking her for her kindness.

"Look, your log still has glowing ember," one American soldier said.

"It is the spirits of the forest protecting us!" exclaimed Mother. "I only hope they will continue to protect each of you until you have reached your own homeland."

The American soldiers then shook hands with the German. There were no words exchanged between them, but they each understood that for this one Christmas Eve they had been united in brotherly love. Tomorrow they might once again be shooting at each other, but today they were one.

The American soldiers turned to the right, and the German soldier to the left. They looked over their shoulders and waved at Dacquiri and her family. She turned and went back to the smoldering yule log and said a silent prayer: "Bless the soldiers that they will no longer fight, that they will return home to their families, and bless Father that he will soon be safely home with us again." ❄

RECIPE
SANDWICH YULE LOG

1 loaf French bread

2 C. cheddar cheese, 1/4" cubes

2 C. fully cooked ham (or best with processed
  pork luncheon meat), 1/4" cubes

1/2 C. onion, finely chopped

1/2 C. margarine, melted

2 Tbs. lemon juice

2 Tbs. poppy seeds

2 tsp. prepared mustard

Slice bread diagonally every 1/2 inch, being careful not to cut through the bottom crust. Place loaf on a piece of foil large enough to wrap completely. Insert cheese, ham, and onion evenly between every other slice. Combine remaining ingredients and drizzle mixture over the top. Wrap in foil tightly and bake at 350 degrees for 30 minutes. Cut bread between unstuffed slices and serve.

CRAFT
FAMILY YULE LOG

1 large round log, selected by family from
  woodpile or forest

1 bottle fantasy snow (spray snow will work,
  but will not glitter or clump)

Picks, ribbons, and decorations of your choice.

Clean off log but leave cracked wood, burls, etc., to give a natural look. Clump or spray snow on log (be sure to do this over a newspaper or mat). Let dry and decorate in any fashion you like; make decorations easy to remove. Burn log on Christmas Eve.

GAME/ACTIVITY
YULE LOG NESTING

Paper slips each with the name of a
  different forest animal

Pins

Explain to everyone that they are all yule logs and that each of them is a home to a forest animal. Then pin a slip of paper on each person's back, animal name facing out. The object of the game is for each person to ask yes-and-no questions of other members until he/she discovers the identity of the animal on his/her back.

Suggestions for animals: bird, deer, squirrel, raccoon, bear, caterpillar, etc.

DAY 3
ANGEL

Angels are heavenly messengers who were selected on the special night of Jesus' birth to announce to the world his coming. Angels come in all shapes and forms, giving meaning to our lives and helping us overcome fears of the unknown. Guardian angels, archangels, cherub angels—all hold a promise of good, and all announce the love of a small baby born in Bethlehem so many years ago.

THE CHRISTMAS ROSE

Anonymous

One dark winter's night, a group of shepherds sat in a field, keeping watch over their flock of sheep. Suddenly an angel appeared to them and all around there shone a great, heavenly light which frightened them very much. But the angel said, "Do not be afraid, for I bring you joyous news. In the city of David, a baby has been born who is the son of God. And this shall be a sign to you. You will find the baby wrapped in swaddling clothes and lying in a manger."

With this message, the angel suddenly was surrounded by a multitude of heavenly hosts, all praising God and saying, "Glory to God in the highest, and on earth, peace and good will toward men."

A great confusion began among the shepherds and the angels. Amidst cries of wonder and astonishment, each was looking through his goods for a gift suitable to bring the baby king. Offerings of bread, blankets, wool, and lambs were gathered by the shepherds as gifts. Beautiful songs, halos, and rays of light were gathered by the angels who prepared to visit the baby. Only a small, very young angel stood still and silent as all hustled about her.

With her halo askew, the little angel gazed sadly around her. She had no one to help her prepare a gift for baby Jesus. Still, she longed to see the wondrous child. Even without a gift, she decided, she would go to the Bethlehem stable. Hopefully no one would notice her.

The lowly stable was not far. The shepherds and other angels approached quietly and joyfully. There, lying upon the sweet-smelling hay, was the baby, only hours old. His eyes were closed and he was warmly wrapped in swaddling clothes. The soft murmuring of his breath made him seem asleep, and a warm glow filled the humble wooden shed.

The little angel's heart swelled at the sight

of him so small and sweet and tender. Oh, how she longed to give him something. He was so beautiful, her eyes filled with tears. One teardrop spilled over, ran down her faint cheek and splashed to the ground. She looked down and beheld, at her feet, a pale flower where the tear had fallen. Gladly she picked it and went to lay it down by the child's head. As she approached, the baby's eyes blinked. His tiny fingers reached up and touched the flower, which turned a blushing rose pink, a Christmas rose.

The baby in the manger and the angel by his side gazed joyfully at each other. The little angel touched the flower. In her heart she knew it was the least of the miracles that happened that night. ❋

RECIPE
LEMON ANGEL PASTA

1 pkg. vegetable stir-fry with asparagus

2 Tbs. margarine

3/4 C. Parmesan cheese, grated

2 C. half-and-half

1 can clams, chopped or minced

2 Tbs. parsley, chopped

2-1/2 tsp. lemon peel, grated

1 C. milk

Salt

Pepper

1 6-oz. pkg. angel hair pasta

Put 3 quarts water in saucepan, place on burner on stove to boil. Sauté vegetables in margarine just until heated. Add 2 cups half-and-half, lemon peel, clams, Parmesan cheese, milk, salt, and pepper. Simmer 10 minutes; to retain color, do not overcook. During this time, cook pasta in boiling water as directed on package. Serve sauce over cooked pasta.

CRAFT
ANGEL PLACE CARDS

This is a simple project for all ages:

Poster paper

Crayons or colored markers

Pearl strips/ribbon

Glue

Popsicle sticks

(1) 10" piece of raffia

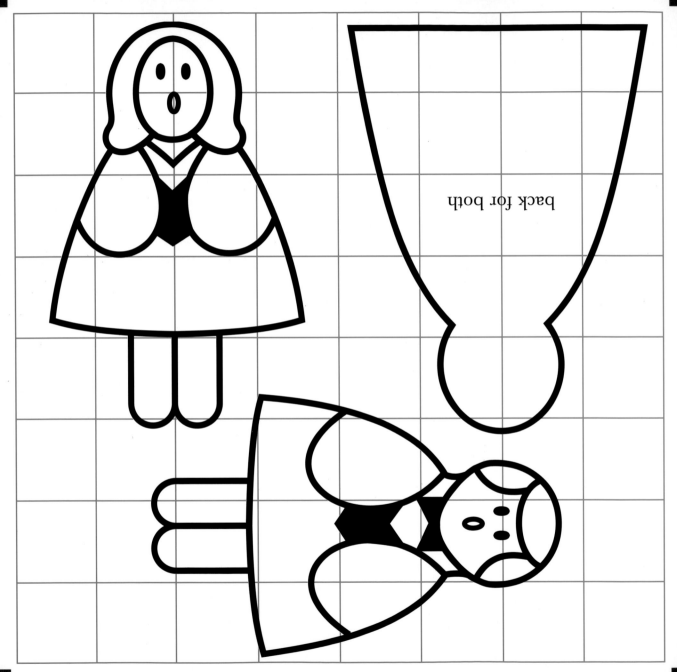

back for both

Copy patterns and transfer on to poster paper. Cut out. Color and glue ribbon (or pearls) to bottom of girl angels. Write names at bottom of each angel. Use crayons or markers to draw on clothes, hair, and faces of angels. Have fun personalizing them to fit the angel in your group. Glue wooden sticks to back of angel front for legs. Make a small bow out of raffia and glue to back of angel front. Add angel back, gluing to bow and top of the front of the angel.

Divide group into two teams. The teams take positions on opposite sides of the sheet, holding it out tight. Place a ping-pong ball in the middle of the sheet, and all players on both teams begin blowing on the ping-pong ball. The object of the game is to blow the ping-pong ball off on the opponent's side. Each time this is done, the team who blew it off scores a point. The team who reaches 15 points wins.

GAME/ACTIVITY
ANGELS IN A CLOUD

1 sheet, any size
1 ping-pong ball (optional: paint angel
    face on ball)

DAY 2 REINDEER

Reindeer help Santa carry out his mission of bringing gifts to the eager girls and boys of the world. In early days Santa had a horse to help him make his visit, but he soon found that reindeer were more practical when delivering to the Scandinavian and Arctic regions. In "The Night Before Christmas," Clement Moore describes Santa and his eight tiny reindeer, calling each of them by name. Then, in 1939, an unusual reindeer was introduced to the children of the world, one with a bright shiny nose–Rudolph.

SANTA'S DILEMMA: THE BIG FOG

by Charlotte Argyle and Taffy Davidson

Adapted from *Rudolph, the Red Nosed Reindeer* by Robert L. May, © 1939, 1967 by Robert L. May Company. Published by *Modern Curriculum Press*, Simon & Schuster Elementary. Used by permission.

Can you imagine a time without Rudolph? A time without a reindeer with a bright red nose to guide Santa's sleigh? Oh, there would be Comet, Cupid, Donner, and Blitzen . . . even Dasher, Dancer, Prancer, and Vixen–but there would be no Rudolph!

For many years, Santa managed just fine with his crew of eight tiny reindeer; but early in December 1939, a terrible fog settled in all around the world. Santa waited anxiously for the fog to lift, but every day it got thicker, and the jolly old man's spirit began to falter. By December 20, he was in a real dilemma.

"What shall I do? Dear me, what will the little boys and girls say if I can't deliver their packages this Christmas Eve?" he asked Mrs. Claus.

"I don't know what you're going to do, but I do know that you will not go out in this fog on Christmas Eve," said Mrs. Claus. "It would be too dangerous for you and the reindeer, and I just can't allow you to take that risk. The children will just have to understand."

Santa knew she was right. He couldn't possibly take the chance of hurting his reindeer, but he didn't think the children would understand if he didn't come to their homes. He decided to ask his smartest elf, Kelly, for a solution to this problem.

"Kelly, what am I going to do? This fog is getting worse every day, and if it doesn't lift by Christmas Eve, I won't be able to make my yearly flight. If I don't make my flight, I'll disappoint all the little boys and girls who have worked all year long at being good so that I'll bring them presents."

Kelly thought long and hard before she answered Santa. "I know a very smart man who is a copywriter for a large department store. If there is anyone bright and creative enough to help you with this problem, it's him," said Kelly.

"Well, who is this man, and where does he live, and how do I get hold of him, and will he . . ."

"Whoa, Santa! Don't get so worked up! I'm sure he'll help you. His name is Robert May, and he lives in Chicago," reassured Kelly. "If you check your back lists, you'll see that you visited him every year because he was always a good little boy. Let's get on the telephone and call him right now."

Santa waited anxiously for someone to answer the telephone on the other end of the line. After seven rings, a small voice answered, "Hello, this is the May residence."

"Who am I speaking to?" asked Santa.

The little girl on the other end of the phone answered, "Barbara."

"Well, Barbara, this is Santa, and I need to talk with your father. It is very important." Within a few minutes, Santa had explained his dilemma to Robert.

"I have just the solution," answered Robert. "I was just telling my daughter, Barbara, a story about a special reindeer who lives at the North Pole. I wrote this reindeer story for the company I work for; they wanted something new to give to the boys and girls who came to visit our toy department during the holidays. I'm sure that this reindeer would be glad to help you."

"But, if you wrote this story, then does this special reindeer exist?" asked Santa, worriedly.

Santa could almost see Robert smile as he answered, "Once something is in writing, isn't it real?"

Immediately, Santa saw the logic in this. "Tell me more about this reindeer!" exclaimed Santa.

Robert explained that the reindeer had a bright shiny nose that would be perfect in helping guide Santa's sleigh through the fog. He said the reindeer's name was Rudolph and that he was probably off playing reindeer games by himself. Santa thanked Robert for his help and told the writer to watch for him and his reindeer on Christmas Eve.

As soon as Santa hung up, he instructed Kelly to get the word out, to use the polar network to find this unusual reindeer. Kelly organized elves and reindeer the pole over to look for Rudolph. Finally, at noon on December 24, Kelly and a band of elves found Rudolph sleeping in an ice cave. They all thought he was wonderful and convinced him to come with them to Santa's workshop.

"You are just what we need!" exclaimed Santa. "You are unique—wonderfully unique! Will you please guide my sleigh tonight as I make my rounds?" he asked.

Rudolph readily agreed, and everyone cheered in excitement. Christmas was saved, all because of this unusual reindeer and the creative copywriter in Chicago.

Well, as we all know, that flight was successful on Christmas Eve in 1939; by 1947, millions of people had read the story created by Robert May. Rudolph became the most famous reindeer in the world, and children of all ages learned from him that even if someone is different or strange, everyone has gifts within themselves that they can share. Even now, children and adults alike wait up anxiously on Christmas Eve, watching for a small red light on the horizon. This tells them that Rudolph, Santa, and his eight tiny reindeer are on their way. ❄

Authors' note: In 1939, Robert May created *Rudolph, the Red Nosed Reindeer* for the Montgomery Ward Company as a Christmas promotion and giveaway for its toy departments. By 1947, over six million copies of the story were in circulation; Rudolph was later immortalized in song by Gene Autry.

Barbara May Lewis is the daughter of Robert May and was four years old at the time her father wrote about Rudolph. She recalls sitting on her father's lap in the evenings as he repeated stories to her, many of which he made up. One of his favorite traditional stories was "The Ugly Duckling," which he loved because the outsider was triumphant. We wish to thank Barbara for sharing this story with us, and for sharing her father and his Rudolph with the rest of the world. Christmas would not be the same without him.

RECIPE
REINDEER OATS

2 C. sugar

1 square margarine

1/2 C. milk, canned

1/4 C. cocoa powder

1 tsp. vanilla

3 C. quick oatmeal

1 C. miniature marshmallows, colored

1/2 C. peanut butter (optional)

1/2 C. coconut (optional)

Put first four ingredients into saucepan and bring to a boil for 2 minutes. Stir constantly. Remove from heat and add vanilla and oatmeal. Let cool slightly, then add marshmallows. Add peanut butter and/or coconut if desired. Stir well and drop by tablespoons onto waxed paper.

REINDEER PEAR SALAD

1 head leaf lettuce

Cottage cheese

1 large can of pears (for head)

Raisins (for eyes)

Maraschino cherries (for nose)

Celery sticks with leaves (for antlers)

Wash lettuce leaves and lay on individual salad plates. Add one scoop of cottage cheese. Drain pears and place one, smooth side up, on each scoop of cottage cheese. Place raisins for eyes and a cherry for the nose. Celery sticks should be about 3 inches long. Split three times, leaving about 1/2 inch at base of stick.

CRAFT
RUDOLPH CENTERPIECE

5 wooden spoons

4 pieces felt–tan, red, green, dark brown

(2) 2" pom-poms, tan

(2) 1" pom-poms, brown

(1) 1/4" pom-pom, red

12 in. gold braid

(2) 15mm oval eyes

1 pipe cleaner

1 yd. ribbon, your choice of color

Holly, bells, etc., for decoration

Craft glue or glue gun

Cut off one spoon handle 1 inch from bowl of spoon. Cut off four spoon handles 4 inches from bowl of spoon.

Use the pattern on the next page to cut felt pieces as follows: tan–4 antlers; red–1 large saddle; green–1 small saddle; dark brown–2 ears.

Legs: glue two tips of long-handled spoon bowls together; repeat.

Body: glue tan pom-poms between spoon bowls.

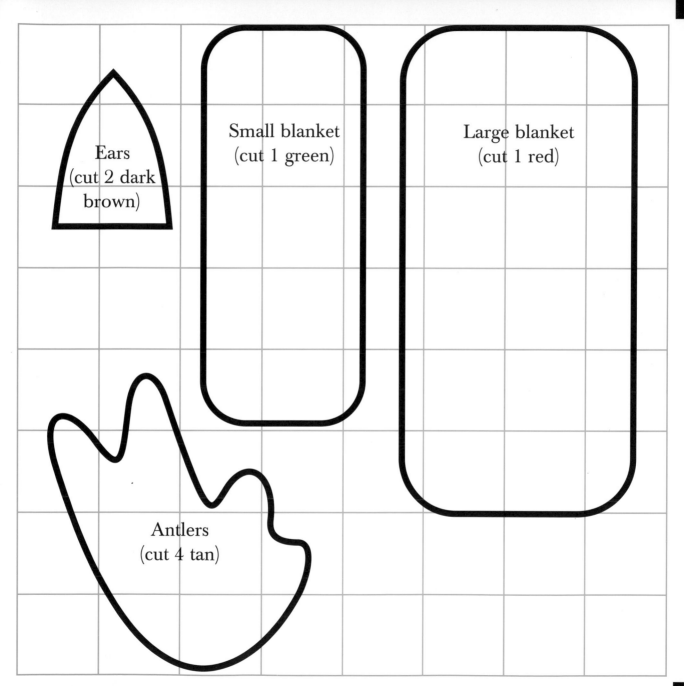

Ears
(cut 2 dark brown)

Small blanket
(cut 1 green)

Large blanket
(cut 1 red)

Antlers
(cut 4 tan)

VEELS

HSREDA

DENSIH

DOLRUHQ

NXEIV

NARRQAE

NDCARE

TLARIE

PDUIK

LOOTRAINED

Saddle: glue smaller green saddle on top of larger red saddle; glue gold braid around edge of green saddle, 1/4 inch from edge.

Head: glue ears onto back of bowl of remaining shorter spoon; then glue antlers behind ears.

Face: glue eyes and brown pom-pom in place on spoon front; glue red pom-pom to center of brown one for nose.

Attach head spoon by applying glue to remaining handle and pushing down into front tan pom-pom (body). Run pipe cleaner under legs, around pom-poms, and tie securely at neck. This will help stabilize head. Glue brown pom-pom tail onto back leg spoons.

Cover back of reindeer with saddle and glue in place. Use ribbon and other decorations for collar on reindeer to cover where head spoon is inserted in body.

GAME/ACTIVITY
REINDEER SCRAMBLE

Use the following scrambled words or make up words of your own. Put these on a sheet of paper and make enough copies for

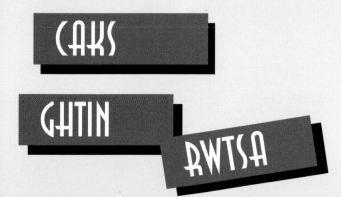

NDOREN

SNPERETS

SSHRCTIMA

LTZBINE

TMCEO

LNRETSA

NCRSI

OVHOES

OOOTRPF

NAATS

LLBES

CAKS

GHTIN

RWTSA

each person present. Be sure everyone gets a pen or pencil. Put a two-minute time limit on the game. The winner is the person who unscrambles the most words. All of these words pertain to reindeer and Christmas.

dolruhp (Rudolph)
hslieg (sleigh)
ndoren (Donner)
snperets (presents)
ltzbine (Blitzen)
hsreda (Dasher)
rwtsa (straw)
ovhoes (hooves)
nxeiv (Vixen)
ncrsi (reins)
tmceo (Comet)
pduic (Cupid)
veels (elves)

ghtin (night)
lootrhnep (Northpole)
lnretsa (antlers)
naats (Santa)
tlarhe (halter)
oootrpf (rooftop)
llbes (bells)
caks (sack)
ndcare (Dancer)
nrrcpac (Prancer)
sshrctima (Christmas)

DAY STAR

The mystery of the Star of Bethlehem has never been solved. Was it a comet or meteorite, or maybe the alignment of two planets? The one thing we do know is that it did exist and was recorded in history. Many believe this star was a heavenly sign of prophecy that, ages ago, fulfilled the shining hope of mankind. Many years ago, wise men followed that star in the East looking for Jesus. That is exactly what wise men are doing today—they are still looking for Jesus and the love he brought to mankind.

SPECIAL MISSION

by Charlotte Argyle and Taffy Davidson

All the stars had gathered, for this was the moment they had been waiting for. The Father of the Heavens had called them together to give them names and assignments. Each was excited, and they chattered nervously among themselves. Finally the moment came, and the heavenly messengers began to line up the stars in a quiet and orderly fashion. One by one the stars approached the Father of the Heavens' podium. He looked down upon them, gave them a name, and explained the new name's meaning. Then he would assign them to constellations, clusters, and moons the universe over.

This was a long, slow process, and the waiting stars became anxious. A few of them crept forward and crowded in line. Others point-bowed (much like elbowed) each other out of line. A clear, shiny, little star stood her ground in line, but she was not very pleased with some of the bigger stars. Then she noticed another little star, not quite as bright, standing off to the side crying.

"What's wrong, little friend?" asked the little star.

"I was in the front of the line, and the big stars pushed and shoved me out of line. Now I will never have a name or an assignment," said the other star.

"Well, come get in line with me," said the little star.

"Now just a minute!" roared the medium star behind the little star. "No crowding in front of me!" Tears formed in the eyes of the little star's new friend.

"It's okay," the little star said. "You take my place, and I'll move to the back of the line." Before her new friend could argue, the little star moved to the very back of the line.

As the little star's new friend reached the podium, the little star listened carefully to the assignment that might have been hers.

"Your name shall be Gordon, and you are assigned to the great constellation Cassiopeia," announced the Father of the Heavens.

"Oh, that could have been me!" exclaimed the little star, but still she patiently awaited her turn at the end of the line. Finally, the little star's turn came. "You shall be named Crystal—only I will spell that K-r-y-s-t-l-e," said the Father of the Heavens. "You are crystal clear and bright. I have chosen a different spelling of this name, however, because kindness begins with a "k," and I saw the kind deed you performed towards Gordon." The little star—now known as Krystle—glowed with warmth. "Further, I know you want to be the brightest star in the Heavens, so I grant you that wish because of your kindness. Unfortunately, however, I have no more constellations to form, and no room in which to place you permanently in the night skies at this time. You will serve a grand mission in the future, but you will have to continue to be patient and wait."

Krystle was very disappointed, but she loved her new name and the fact that she was the brightest little star in the Heavens. She knew that someday she would shine over her own country, or maybe even the world, and that she would be splendid.

Centuries passed, and one by one the other stars were called upon to fill their missions. The stars who had not yet taken up their permanent residences spent their days playing games such as "shooting stars" or "asteroid catch." No one liked to play shooting stars with Krystle because she was so bright that she was the only one people on earth would notice shooting across the skies. The others were very jealous. When they played catch with Krystle, her brightness blinded them, and they could never catch the asteroids, so Krystle always won. Eventually they began sneaking away without her, or not asking her to play at all. Gordon never forgot Krystle's kindness though, and he stayed and played with her, no matter what.

One day while Krystle and Gordon were playing by themselves, a messenger from the Father of the Heavens came and told Gordon it was his time to join the constellation Cassiopeia. Krystle was happy for her friend and glowed brightly for him, but after Gordon left, Krystle was lonely. Eventually, one by one, all the stars were called to join their new homes, and Krystle was all alone.

One day the Father of the Heavens himself came to Krystle and told her it was her time to appear in the night skies above earth, and that it was time for her to glow her very brightest. She soon arrived at her new home, but she was immediately filled with disappointment. Her mission was not to shine on a country, but only to shine on a small town—in fact, on the outskirts of one small town.

Krystle no longer felt patient or kind. She was angry and did not want to be so bright; she wanted to belong to her own constellation. As she looked down on the lowly stable, she saw a glow. As she looked closer, the glow became brighter and brighter, and she noticed that is was coming from a small, newborn baby. She then realized what her special mission was, and she glowed with all her might. Even as she glowed, she knew her light was no match for the light the child would give the world. She was so happy. Her mission was to shine light on the Savior of the world, who in turn would shine light on mankind. As she made her own light brighter, she was seen in other countries, on other continents, and she led the wise men and shepherds to the stable where the baby lay.

Soon the baby and his parents had to leave the stable, and Krystle was feeling very lonely again. The Father of the Heavens came to her and said, "Krystle, you have filled your great mission. Your light has been seen by many and will continue to be seen in the hearts of those who reflect on this night for generations. You will no longer be as visible to them, shining your light on this stable, but you will always be with them.

"I have arranged for you to be in a cluster in the center of Cassiopeia. No one can quite see them, but with your crystal-clear beauty they will see the whole cluster. Further, I have arranged for you to be dimmer, so your companions will enjoy your beauty. But best of all, you'll be right next to Gordon."

Krystle glowed with happiness.

To this day, on a clear night in the northern hemisphere, you can see a small cluster with a crystal-clear star glowing in the warmth of Cassiopeia's arms. ❊

RECIPE
SAUSAGE STARS

1 lb. sausage, ground

1-1/2 C. cheddar cheese, grated

1-1/2 C. Monterey jack cheese, grated

1 C. ranch dressing

1 small can black olives, sliced

1/2 C. sweet pepper, chopped (red or green)

Vegetable oil

1 pkg. frozen wonton wrappers

Crumble sausage and cook; drain. Preheat oven to 350 degrees. Combine cheeses, dressing, olives and peppers with sausage. Grease muffin tins and press one wrapper in each cup, forming a star. Fill with sausage mixture and bake 10 minutes until bubbly.

CRAFT
STAR BOOK COVER

This project may be hot-glued, hand- or machine-sewn.

Book to be covered
Pinking shears
Fabric of your choice
3/4"-wide lace, to go around book
   when opened up
Star cut-out of solid material from pattern (size
   up or down for book)
Trim for star
Glue gun

Lay open book on fabric and trim, leaving 1/2 inch on top and bottom edges of book. On the length, leave 2 inches to make pocket to slip book into. Overstitch or zigzag stitch around complete edge of book cover. Turn pockets to inside and glue at top and bottom edges. Place book in cover and then glue lace around edges of cover. Center star in middle of book and trim as desired. This is a good project for covering an old Bible, a worn-out book, or a new journal. You can personalize the cover by cross-stitching a name on the star.

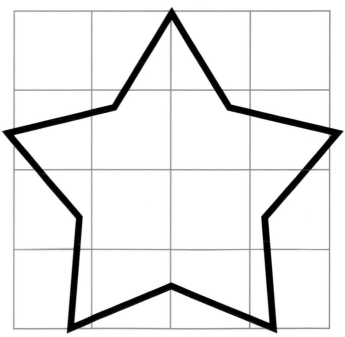

GAME/ACTIVITY
STARGAZER

1 flashlight
Provide the following for each person:
(1) 8 1/2"-by-11" piece of construction
  paper, black
1 pencil or pen

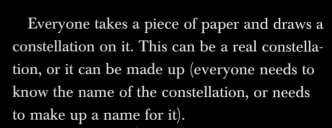

Everyone takes a piece of paper and draws a constellation on it. This can be a real constellation, or it can be made up (everyone needs to know the name of the constellation, or needs to make up a name for it).

Using the sharp end of the pencil or pen, poke holes through the paper where each star of the constellation appears. When completed, turn off all the lights. Hold paper up and shine flashlight through holes so that the star images appear on a blank wall. Each person then tells the group the name of his/her constellation and any information known or made up about it.